Buddhism:

A Brief Introduction

**Based on the Compassionate Teachings
of the
Venerable Tripitaka Master Hsuan Hua**

by the Faculty of the
Developing Virtue Secondary School
Sagely City of 10,000 Buddhas
Talmage, California.

Buddhist Text Translation Society
Dharma Realm Buddhist University
Dharma Realm Buddhist Association
Burlingame, California U.S.A.

Buddhism: A Brief Introduction

Published by:
Buddhist Text Translation Society
1777 Murchison Drive, Burlingame, CA 94010-4504

First edition published June 1996: commemorating the 20th anniversary of the founding of the Sagely City of Ten Thousand Buddhas and Gold Wheel Sagely Monastery.

Printed in the United States of America
Reprinted in Malaysia August 1998

04 03 02 01 00 99 98 97 96   10 9 8 7 6 5 4 3 2 1
ISBN 0-88139-517-X

Unconditional Lovingkindness & Compassion

At that time the Thus Come One (the Buddha) by means of his unobstructed pure "eye of wisdom", contemplated all living beings everywhere in the Dharma-realm and said this:

Amazing! Truly amazing! How it is that all of these living beings are replete with the Thus Come One's wisdom. Yet they are ignorant and confused, and do not know or see it. I should teach them the Holy Path, to cause them to forever separate from false thinking and attachments, so that they will see the Thus Come One's vast wisdom within themselves, which is no different from the Buddha.

At that time he taught these living beings to cultivate the Holy Path, and caused them to be apart from false thinking. After they separated from false thinking they realized the Thus Come One's measureless wisdom. Thus he benefited and brought peace and happiness to all living beings.

(Words spoken by the Buddha upon his Complete Enlightenment as recorded in the *Manifestations of the Thus Come One*, Chapter 37, *Flower Adornment Sutra*)

Contents

Illustrations

Preface

Many books have been written to introduce the Buddha's teachings. Why write another one? There are three main reasons for compiling another work of this kind. These reasons also help to define the uniqueness of this book.

First, this book relies primarily on translations of source materials, rather than narrative explanations and interpretations of the teachings. Most introductory books on Buddhism are written in the second person and not in the Buddha's own words. Primary source materials such as the Sutras[1] (discourses by the Buddha or his contemporary disciples) appear infrequently, if at all, in most of the literature. This is understandable, because it makes for easier reading. Somewhat more energy and concentration is required to read original sources, because they tend to be more solemn in tone and rich in meaning. However, reading the Sutras directly yields unexpected treasures. One encounters the actual teaching of the Master unfiltered through someone else's personal views. Therefore, the reader has the freedom to discover his own meanings and draw his own conclusions from the teachings. *Buddhism: A Brief Introduction* tries to let the Buddha speak for himself directly to the reader by way of brief Sutra passages presented in a manner that weaves the entire body of teachings into a coherent whole.

Second, this small book is distinctive in its attempt to blend the central teachings of the various schools and sects of Buddhism into a unified and cogent philosophy. Thus the reader is being introduced to the fundamental teachings accepted by all major schools of Buddhism. With the intertwining of the Four Noble Truths, the paramount teaching of the Theravada or Southern

Tradition, and the Bodhisattva's Four Magnificent Vows, the essential teaching of the Mahayana or Northern Tradition, a universal Buddhism emerges. This single, unified Buddhism combines the practical wisdom of the Sages with the all encompassing compassion of the Bodhisattvas. The result is a very complete and compelling Buddhism.

The third special quality of this book is its vitality. The quotations taken directly from source materials convey the spirit and purpose of the Buddha's teaching immediately to the reader. Unfortunately, many modern works on Buddhism, in the name of "scholarly objectivity", treat the Buddha's teachings as an academic discipline such as sociology, anthropology, and other social sciences. Here in the realm of wisdom and spiritual insight, however, scholarly interpretations are often inadequate and strangely out of place. Extensive linguistic analysis, archaeological finds, and social analysis may lead to a better understanding of the cultural context within which the Buddha lived and taught, but they offer us, almost no insight into the profound meaning and abiding truths that continue to pulse through these timeless teachings. And in some ways mere scholarship can often inadvertently "miss the forest for the trees". From the outset of his career, the Buddha explained that his teachings were "only a finger pointing at the moon; not the moon itself". That is, they were a means or way to be cultivated, not a creed to be believed or a dogma to cling to. You must "drink the water yourself, to know whether it is warm or cold" — see for yourself what is true and attain ultimate freedom from suffering. Thus the Buddha said:

Monks, do you not speak that which is known by yourselves, seen by yourselves, discovered by yourselves?

Yes, Venerable Sir.

*You, Monks, have been instructed by this Dharma
(teaching) which is evident, timeless, inviting one to come
and see, leading onwards, and to be personally known
by the wise.*[2]

The implication is clear: without actually practicing the teachings
it is not possible to fully comprehend them. Mere study cannot
compare to actual practice and direct experience. Thus, in the
Bodhisattvas Ask For Clarification, Chapter 10, *Flower Adornment
Sutra*, we find this principle stated in the following vivid analogies:

*Like a physician who,
though skillful in prescribing medicine,
Is unable to cure his own illness;
Without practicing the Dharma,
Much study is the same way.*

*Like one who counts the wealth of others'
But has not a penny of his own;
Without practicing the Dharma,
Much study is the same way.*

*Like a person born in a King's palace,
Who still suffers hunger and cold;
Without practicing the Dharma,
Much study is the same way.*

*Like a deaf musician playing tunes
Others enjoy but he himself does not hear;
Without practicing the Dharma,
Much study is the same way.*

Like a blind artist whose many drawings
Are displayed for others,
but he himself can never see;
Without practicing the Dharma,
Much study is the same way.

Introduction

If one wishes to fully understand
All Buddhas of the past, present, and future,
One should contemplate the nature of the Dharma Realm[3]:
Everything is only a creation of the mind.[4]

"Who and what am I?" "Why do I exist?" Each of us, during some part of our life, wonders about these questions. While we're aware of our own being, we don't actually know how or why we came to be. Our existence poses a great mystery. Our views of who we are and why we're here, consciously or unconsciously, affect every moment of our lives. The Buddha was both troubled and fascinated by these questions. He was troubled, in that life unexamined, unsolved seemed meaningless; he was fascinated, in that the solution to this deep riddle was accessible, within reach, almost beckoning.

The teaching of the Buddha, known as the Dharma, grew out of his personal discovery, his awakening to "things as they really are." Indeed, the word Dharma literally translated is "law", meaning the universal laws that govern all of reality. These laws are eternal. A Buddha is merely a human being who discovers these laws of reality and compassionately makes them known for others. Buddhism explains the mystery of existence in a way that we can both understand and not understand. This was for a reason: enlightenment must be directly experienced, not simply explained. Properly taught, it should awaken in us a sense of great wonder; a resolve to seek enlightenment ourselves. The Buddha taught that:

1. All of existence is a creation of the mind. The true nature of

our mind has no particular location in space and no beginning or end in time. It is not born and does not die. The realization of this true nature is known as Nirvana[5] — something so profound and extraordinary that it cannot be described in words or conceived in thought. It can only be known by direct realization. Because of its profundity, the Buddha spoke of Nirvana in terms of what it is not:

> *There is, Monks, that realm, wherein there is no earth, no water, no fire, no air, no sphere of infinite space, no sphere of infinite consciousness, no sphere of nothingness, no sphere of thought nor lack of thought[6]. There is not this world or a world beyond, or both together, or sun or moon. This, I say, Monks, has no coming, no going, no staying, no passing away, and no arising without support; without duration and without any basis. This, indeed, is the end of suffering.[7]*

2. Because of ignorance we experience our "self"within Samsara[8], the realm of birth and death. This unreal "self" undergoes limitless suffering. This suffering is perpetuated life after life as long as we thirst for the pleasures of existence in Samsara.

3. The purpose of the Buddha's teaching is to point the way to the elimination of ignorance that covers over our true nature. Once we have awakened to it, out of great compassion, we strive to help all beings to also awaken to their true nature; to liberate all that lives. Thus, personal enlightenment and universal enlightenment, self and others, become one and the same.

> *When you can see that the mountains, the rivers, the great earth and all that originates from them, are things*

within your own inherent nature; that the Three Realms of Existence are only the mind, and that the myriad dharmas are only consciousness; once you attain that state, then everything, every phenomenon is devoid of origination and cessation. Everything you see — the mountains, the rivers, the great earth, the plants are all one true Reality.[9]

The Four Noble Truths &
The Bodhisattva's Four Magnificent Vows

In the Buddha's teaching, the problem of existence and its solution are precisely expressed in the Four Noble Truths and the corresponding Bodhisattva's Four Magnificent Vows. The Four Noble Truths are best described by an analogy. The First Truth diagnoses the symptom of an illness and the Second determines its cause. The Third Truth describes the final cure of the disease once the cause has been eliminated, and the Fourth prescribes the medicine or treatment that will bring about the cure. The Four Magnificent Vows extend these same truths beyond oneself to include all living beings. Thus in numerous discourses the Buddha said:

> *Formerly and now, also, it is just suffering and the cessation of suffering that I teach.*[10]

Bodhisattva is a Sanskrit word. It is a compound made up of the two words: *bodhi* which means "awakened" or "enlightened"; and *sattva* which means "being". A Bodhisattva is both an "awakened being" and "one who awakens beings". He is one imbued with great wisdom and compassion who simultaneously *strives to perfect* his own awakening along with his ability to awaken all other living beings. When the Bodhisattva has totally perfected these, he becomes a Buddha, one *already perfected* in wisdom and compassion.

Part I of *Buddhism: A Brief Introduction* is divided into chapters on each of the Four Truths and Vows. A final chapter explains the meaning of Sangha. Each chapter begins with passages from the Sutras to illustrate each of the Vows and Truths.

BTTS = a publication by the Buddhist Text Translation Society which is available to the public.

[1]"Sutra" literally means a "string" or "thread". Important words or brief phrases in religious teachings strung together were thus called Sutras by analogy with the string or thread with which a garland of flowers is made. All Buddhist Sutras were transmitted orally for the first three to four hundred years after the Buddha passed into ultimate Nirvana. The teachings were originally taught in the various dialects of the people. In about the second or first century BC the Sutras started to be written down in various Indic-languages. The largest collection of Sutras in the Theravada or Southern Tradition of Buddhism has survived in the Pali language. The Pali Canon consists of five groups of Sutras called Nikayas. The Northern Tradition was originally recorded in Sanskrit and Sanskrit derivative languages. However, a very small fraction of these have survived to this present time in Sanskrit. Fortunately, ancient monk-scholars from India and China began to translate the Sutras of the Northern Tradition into Chinese beginning in approximately the first century AD. Through their work, which lasted for many centuries, the vast majority of Mahayana Sutras have survived in Chinese.

[2]*Majjhima Nikaya I* 265.

[3]"Dharma Realm" is special term in Buddhism which most closely corresponds to the meaning of "reality". "*Dharma*" has three basic meanings. 1) "Law", which refers to the Buddha's teachings in which he reveals the universal laws or truths that govern all of reality. In this sense of the Buddha's teachings, it especially refers to the spiritual practices he taught. 2) "Duty" refers specifically to one's duty in life in accordance with one's station, or it can mean one's religious or spiritual duty. 3) a "thing" or "phenomenon" in the broadest sense. The Dharma Realm is the totality of the realm of all beings and states and the complex ways in which they interact and interpenetrate. It is the whole limitless universe. The nature of the Dharma Realm is the true mind of all living beings. Our true mind pervades the entire Dharma Realm, and the Dharma Realm is not apart from our true mind.

[4]*Praises in the Suyama Heaven*, Chapter 20, *Flower Adornment Sutra*.

[5]*nir* means "not" and *vana* is literally "effort of blowing". The origin of the word probably refers to a smith's fire, which "goes out" or "becomes extinguished" if no longer blown on by the bellows. A frequent simile is that of a lamp's ceasing through exhaustion of wick and oil. The ancient translators of Sanskrit Sutras into Chinese interpreted Nirvana to mean "without

origination or destruction".

[6]These last four spheres are the four heavens in the Formless Realm. Refer to Appendix I: A Chart of *Samsara* (the Realm of Birth and Death).

[7]*Udana, Pataligamiya Vagga, Sutra No. 1.*

[8]Refer to Appendix 1: A Chart of *Samsara* (the Realm of Birth and Death).

[9]Venerable High Master Hsuan Hua's commentary to the *Shurangama Sutra*, Volume 1, BTTS.

[10]*Maha-Parinirvana Sutra* of the Pali Canon.

Part I
The Teachings of Buddhism

Chapter One

Suffering:
The Problem of Existence

First Magnificent Vow of the Bodhisattva:
*I vow to rescue the boundless
living beings from suffering.*

*The Buddha toils through eons for the sake of living beings
Cultivating limitless, oceanic, great compassion.
To comply with living beings, he enters birth and death,
Transforming the multitudes everywhere, so they become pure.*[1]

This vow corresponds to the Noble Truth of Suffering.

*What, Bhikshus, is the Noble Truth of Suffering? Birth
is suffering; old age is suffering; sickness is suffering;
death is suffering; sorrow, lamentation, pain, grief, and
despair are suffering; to be together with what or those
you hate is suffering; to be separated from what or those
you love is suffering; not to obtain what you wish for is
suffering; in general, identification with the Five
Constituents of Existence (physical form, feelings,
thoughts, volitional formations, and consciousness) is
suffering.*[2] The Truth of Suffering should be understood.

To mention the "problem" of existence already implies there is
something wrong with life as we experience it. What is the
problem? The Buddha's own life provides an insight.

The Buddha, Shakyamuni, whose name means "Sage of the Shakya clan," was born about 2500 years ago in Kapilavastu, India. His father was a ruler of one of the many kingdoms comprising India at that time. Upon his birth, seers predicted his son would either become a great world-ruling monarch or would renounce the mundane life to become a fully enlightened sage, a Buddha, who would teach countless living beings to find a genuine happiness that transcends the world.

The king, fearing his son might renounce the throne, took special precautions in his son's upbringing to prevent him from observing the sufferings of the world. His son, the prince, continuously enjoyed the myriad pleasures of life and did not come into contact with any of its pains. Through his youth the Buddha-to-be enjoyed separate palaces for each season. It is said that he never even left the palace grounds. Thus the prince's experience of life resembled a heaven on earth.

At nineteen the prince asked his father if he could take his first excursion outside the palace grounds. The king reluctantly consented but made sure that along the highway his son would encounter no one maimed, aged, or sick.

The prince, however, on his first excursion outside the palace grounds had the following experiences:

Old Age

At that time the king of the Pure Abodes Heaven³ suddenly appeared at the side of the road transfigured as an old, decrepit man in order to stir repugnance in the prince's heart. The prince saw the old man and was startled. He asked his charioteer, "What kind of person is this with white hair and bent-back? His eyes are dim; his body wobbles. He leans on a cane and walks feebly. Has his body changed unexpectedly, or is this just the way things are naturally?

The charioteer's mind wavered. He dared not answer true. Then the god from the Pure Abodes Heaven, with his spiritual powers, caused him to speak truly. "His form's decayed; his energy almost gone. Much distress and little happiness mark his life. Forgetful now, his sense faculties are wasted. These are the attributes of old age. Originally he was a suckling child, long-nurtured at his mother's breast. Then as a youth he cavorted and played about handsome, unrestrained, enjoying sense desires. However, as the years went by, his body withered and decayed. Now old age has brought him to ruin."

The prince heaved a long sigh, and then asked the charioteer, "Is he the only one who has become decrepit and old, or will we all like this become?"

The charioteer answered him again, "This lot in life alike awaits the Venerable One. As time goes on your body will naturally decay. This certainly, without doubt, will come to pass. All those young and energetic, will grow old. This, all in the world know, yet still they seek for pleasure."

The Bodhisattva had long cultivated the karma of purity and wisdom, and widely planted the roots of every virtue. The fruits of his vows were now blossoming. Hearing these words on the suffering of old age, he shivered; his hair stood on end. Like a terrified herd of animals flees the bolt of a thunder clap, the Bodhisattva in the same way trembled with fear, as he deeply sighed and contemplated the suffering of old age.

He shook his head and steadily gazed pondering the agony of old age. "How can people find delight in the pleasures of the world when old age brings it all to ruin? It affects everyone; none escape it. For a time the body may be robust and strong, but everything's subject to change. Now my own eyes behold the truth of old age, how can I not be disgusted and wish to leave it?"

The Bodhisattva told the charioteer, "Quickly turn the chariot around and go back. Unable to forget that old age will call for me, what happiness could I find in these gardens and groves?" Obeying the command, he drove as fast as the wind, and quickly returned to the palace.

The prince mulled over the experience of old age. The palace felt like a desolate graveyard. Everything he touched left him numb and cold. His heart could find no peace. The king heard that his son was unhappy, so he urged him to take another excursion. He ordered all of his officers to make everything more resplendent than before.

Sickness

The god again transformed himself, this time as a sick person, barely holding on to his life at the side of the road. With a gaunt body and bloated stomach, slow, asthmatic breath, stooped with withered hands and legs, he sorrowfully wept and moaned.

The prince asked the charioteer, "What kind of person

is this?" The charioteer answered, "This is a sick person. The four great elements composing his body are completely out of balance. Emaciated and weak he's unable to do much of anything. Tossing back and forth, he has to rely on others."

Hearing this the prince's heart swelled with pity. He then asked, " Is it only this person who gets sick, or are others subject to the same?"

He answered, "In this world everyone will also get diseased. Sickness plagues all who have a body. Yet foolish people seek joy in the fleeting pleasures of the world."

The prince heard this with horror and dismay. His mind and body shuddered like the shimmering moon in troubled water. "Adrift on this ocean of great suffering, how can one be at ease?" He sighed for people in the world, so deluded, confused, and obstructed. "The thief of sickness can come at any time. Yet they seem happy and delighted."

Then he had the chariot turn around and go back, his mind distraught about the woe of sickness. He was just like someone who, about to be beaten, curls his body waiting for the clubs to fall. He quietly stayed in the palace, aspiring only for a happiness beyond the world.

The king inquired the reason for his son's return. He was told the prince had seen a sick person. The king was aghast and totally beside himself. He severely reprimanded the people who had prepared the road. But they too were perplexed and could not explain what had

7

happened.

Then more songstresses were sent to the Prince's harem. Their music was more exquisite than before. The King hoped the prince, enamored by song and dance, would grow infatuated with the world and not abandon the householder's life. Day and night came offerings of lovely women and song, yet he was not happy at all.

The king himself traveled in search of gardens, wondrous and fine. He also selected the most fair and voluptuous maidens for the Prince. They fawned on him; with all their talents served him. They were so stunning, one look at them befuddled men.

He adorned even more the royal road so all impurities were out of sight. He ordered once more the good charioteer, to carefully cleave to the gilded path.

Death

At that time the god from the Pure Abodes Heaven transfigured into a corpse. Four people carrying the cadaver appeared right before the Bodhisattva. Only the Bodhisattva and the charioteer saw this. No one else was aware of it. He asked, "What is this body, with flowers and banners adorned? Those trailing behind are all grief-stricken. Their hair hanging down, they wail as they follow along."

The god again inspired the charioteer. Thus he answered, "This is a dead person. All of his organs have deteriorated; his life has been cut off. His mind has scattered; his consciousness has left. His spirit has departed and his body has withered. It's rigid and straight like dry wood. Formerly all of his relatives and friends adored him. They bathed in mutual affection. Now none of them even wish to see him. They will shun and abandon him in an empty graveyard." When the prince heard of death his heart ached; he felt all bound up. He asked, "Is it only this person who dies, or is everyone in the world destined to the same?"

He answered, "Each and every one must die. Whatever has a beginning, also must end. The old, the young, and those middle aged, anyone who has a body, is subject to decay."

The prince was shocked. His body leaned forward over the railing of the chariot. His breathing halted and he sighed, "Why are people in the world so deluded? Everyone sees that their body will perish, yet they still go through life so casually. They're not insensible like dead wood or stone. Yet they never think about the impermanence of life."

He ordered the charioteer to turn back home "This is no time for a pleasure ride. Life can end at any time. How could I indulge in an excursion?"[4]

These experiences compelled the prince to renounce the common life to find the path beyond birth and death. His father, however, was adamant that he remain in the palace. The prince promised to stay if his father could guarantee four things:

Only under four conditions will I abandon my resolve to leave the householder's life.

Guarantee my life will last forever, that I will be without sickness or old age, and that all my material wealth will never perish. Then I will respect your order and not leave the householder's life.

If these four wishes cannot be fulfilled, let me leave the householder's life. Please do not attempt to thwart me. I am in a burning house. How could you not let me out?[5]

The prince did leave the palace to undertake a spiritual quest to solve the problem of existence. Six years later he became a Buddha, a fully Awakened One.

The Noble Truth of Suffering suggests that a deep malaise permeates our life. Everything that we live for, everything that is dear to us will eventually be lost: our fathers and mothers, our sisters and brothers, our sons and daughters, our husbands or wives, and eventually even our own lives. Death takes everything away. This is a very serious matter both because it is inescapable and real, and moreover because paradoxically the inevitability of death gives direction and meaning to life. The Bodhisattva feels a oneness with and resulting great compassion for all beings who undergo suffering. Thus he follows the Buddha's path to Awakening to help all beings end suffering and attain true happiness.

I will be a good doctor for the sick and suffering. I will lead those who have lost their way to the right road. I will be a bright light for those in the dark night. I will enable the poor and destitute to discover hidden treasures. The Bodhisattva impartially benefits all living beings in this manner....

Why is this? Because all Buddhas, the Thus Come Ones,[6]

take a heart of great compassion as their very substance. Because of living beings they have great compassion. From great compassion the Bodhi-mind is born; and because of the Bodhi-mind[7], they accomplish the Equal and Proper Awakening.[8]

Therefore, great compassion for all the myriad living beings who are suffering in Samsara is the catalyst for making the profound resolution to become a fully Enlightened Buddha, that is, for generating the Bodhi-mind.

The Meritorious Qualities of the Bodhi-Mind

You should know that the Bodhi-mind is completely equal to all the merit and virtue of all dharmas taught by the Buddha. Why? It is because the Bodhi mind produces all practices of the Bodhisattvas. It is because the Thus Comes Ones of the past, present, and future are born from the Bodhi-mind. Therefore, good young man, if there are those who have brought forth the resolve for Anuttara-Samyak-Sambodhi[9], they have already given birth to infinite merit and virtue and are universally able to collect themselves and remain on the path of All-wisdom....

Good young man, it is just the way a single lamp, if brought into a dark room, is able to totally eradicate a hundred thousand years of darkness. The lamp of the Bodhi-mind of the Bodhisattva, Mahasattva[10] is that way too, in that upon its entering the room which is the mind of a living being, the various dark obstacles of all the karmic afflictions[11] from hundreds of quadrillions of ineffable numbers of eons can all be totally destroyed.[12]

11

[1]*Rulers of the World*, Chapter 1, *Flower Adornment Sutra.*

[2]*Turning the Dharma Wheel Sutra, Dhamma Cakka Ppavattana Sutra, Samyutta Nikaya* LVI, 11.

[3]Refer to Appendix 1, Chart of *Samsara*, The Realm of Birth and Death. The Pure Abodes are the Five Heavens of No-Return in the Form Realm.

[4]*Acts of the Buddha (Buddhacharita)*, by Bodhisattva Ashvagosha composed in the 1st century BC or AD.

[5]*ibid.*

[6]"Thus Come One" is one of the ten titles of the Buddha. See Chapter 4 for the entire list of ten.

[7]The Bodhi-mind is the catalyst for the Bodhisattva path. Refer to the section on the Bodhisattva under the heading, "The Sangha of the Sages" in Chapter 5.

[8]*Universal Worthy's Conduct and Vows*, Chapter 40, *Flower Adornment Sutra*, BTTS.

[9]*Anuttara-Samyak-Sambodhi* literally the "Unsurpassed, Right, and Total Enlightenment" meaning the ultimate Enlightenment of a Buddha.

[10]*Mahasattva* literally means "great being", that is, a great *Bodhisattva*.

[11]See Chapter 2 for karma and afflictions.

[12]*Entering the Dharma Realm*, Chapter 39, Volume 8, *Flower Adornment Sutra*, BTTS.

Chapter Two

The Cause of Suffering: Ignorance and Karma

Second Magnificent Vow of the Bodhisattva:
*I vow to put an end to the
infinite afflictions of living beings.*
*Living beings are drowning in the sea of afflictions.
Defiled by deluded and confused views,
they are quite alarming.
The Great Teacher feels pity in his heart and enables
them to separate from afflictions forever.*[1]

This corresponds to the Noble Truth of the Cause of Suffering.

What, Bhikshus, is the Noble Truth of the Cause of Suffering? Just this thirst, leading to being, accompanied by delight and passion, gratifying itself now here and now there; namely the thirst for sense pleasures, the thirst for being, and the thirst for non-being.[2] (This "thirst" implies ignorance of the first truth of suffering. Ignorance and thirst are the most fundamental afflictions.) The Cause of Suffering should be cut off.

To end suffering, we have to recognize its cause. The Buddha found that the fundamental cause of suffering is ignorance. Ignorance in turn leads to the arisal of self-centered desire. Ignorance and desire combine to blind us and preclude any possibility of realizing our inherent spiritual nature. Confused and

13

dazed we "mistake fish eyes for pearls," i.e., confuse the ebb and flow of things impermanent with our true self.

You have lost track of your fundamental treasure: the perfect, wondrous bright mind. And in the midst of your clear and enlightened nature, you mistake the false for the real because of ignorance and delusion.[3]

Your true nature is occluded by the misperception of false appearances based on external objects, and so from beginningless time until the present you have taken a thief for your son. You have thus lost your source eternal and instead turn on the wheel of birth and death.[4]

Because of ignorance, living beings create karma. The word "karma" means "activity." Karma more specifically is activities we do over and over again — activities rooted in desire and governed by the law of cause and effect. The law of cause and effect, simply stated, is that every good or bad act of body, speech and thought, generates a corresponding good or bad result. The cause necessarily brings the result, which differs only in degree and time according to circumstances.

For example, someone berates you, and then you scold him in return. His berating you is the result of past karma which has now come to fruition. When you scold him, you are creating new karma, which will bring equally unpleasant results in the future. All the things *you do* in body, speech and thought are causes. And all the *things that happen to you* are results. Thus, the present is both the fruit of the past and the seed of the future. What you are is what you have done; and, what you do is what you will become.

Karma, however, should not be construed as "fate" or "predestination." Karma is not fixed and unalterable. Only the principle or "law" of karma is unalterable: you reap what you sow. Yet free will and conscious choice are present in and inform each and every action. The individual is free to choose, but not free to evade the consequences of those choices. Once there is action with intention, the results inexorably follow. One cannot escape this immutable law, but one can understand and master its workings and thereby escape the cycle of existence with its endless births and deaths.

Hence one of the major goals of Buddhist practice is to attain the pure conscience and resulting clarity of mind that enables one to make wise choices and avoid errors in cause and effect. Even sages, including Buddhas and Bodhisattvas, are not exempt from the law of cause and effect; they simply do not err in cause and effect. The stress on moral precepts and meditation in Buddhism thus makes sense within the context of karma. Morality and mindfulness are designed to keep us in touch with our actions and, more importantly, the intentions driving those actions. Actions motivated by selfish desire and ignorance invariably result in unwholesome karma and entrapment. The converse is equally true: actions taken free of selfish desire and delusion invariably result in wholesome karma and genuine freedom. Being able to see and intelligently choose between good and evil, wholesome and unwholesome, liberation and bondage is the hallmark of wisdom — one of Buddhism's two greatest virtues.

Compassion, the other central virtue of Buddhist practice, also arises from a clear understanding of karma. The principle of karma implies and confirms a deep interrelationship between all beings and all things. This inter-relatedness among all things means that what touches one, touches all. This is the truth that all Buddhas and Bodhisattvas awaken to. The dichotomies we make between self and others, body and mind, and man and nature are all

15

fabrications and false. We thus, in a very real way, 'do unto ourselves what we do unto others', suggesting yet a deeper dimension of meaning to the long-standing Golden Rule.

Compassion, however, goes beyond instrumental kindness, i.e., being good to others so that they will be good to us. Compassion literally means 'being one with everyone'. It is a way of seeing and being (not merely an attitude or way of thinking) in absolute identity with all that lives. It is both how things really are and how things might be — a solution to all of mankind's conflict and disorder.

Thus, understanding karma is central to understanding Buddhism — the teaching of wisdom and compassion. Karma is the primary force that keeps us turning in the illusory cycle of birth and death. When understood and mastered, it is the same force that can free us from this hapless cycle, and gives us the compassion and wisdom to truly benefit the world. The Buddha gave an analogy for those caught in this cycle of karma:

Bad karma that is created,
like milk, does not curdle at once;
Fermenting, it follows the fool
like a fire covered by ashes.[5]

The family and social environments that we are born into and even our bodies are the result of our karma from past lives. The entire world as well manifests from the collective karma of all living beings.

Living beings' individual karma,
Leads to worlds of infinite kinds.
Therein, of those who grasp at life,
Each receives a different measure

of suffering and happiness.[6]

The reason why people undergo seemingly unwarranted rewards and retributions must ultimately be traced back to causes or "seeds" we planted in the past. We ourselves are responsible for everything that happens to us. Karma is fair, impartial, and never in error.

All the many things you do to others will return to be undergone by yourself.[7]

If you want to know of your past lives' causes,
Look at rewards you are reaping today.
If you wish to know your future lives,
You need but notice what you're doing right now.[8]

All men and women in the world, whether poor and lowly or wealthy and noble, whether they are undergoing limitless sufferings or enjoying blessings without end, are all undergoing retributions from causes in their past lives.[9]

Sometimes people have plentiful goods.
The reason is quite fair.
In the past those same people
Gave food liberally to the poor.
Some happy fellows' fathers and mothers,
Enjoy long life, contentment, and ease.
The reason for rewards such as these, you wonder?
In times past they looked after orphans
And cared for all elderly people as their own.[10]

If he meets those who take life, Earth Store Bodhisattva describes the retribution of a short life. If he meets robbers and petty thieves, he tells of the retribution of poverty and acute suffering.

17

*To those with harsh tongues, he explains they will have
a quarreling family. To people who slander, he warns of
the retribution of a tongueless and cankerous mouth.
And to those angry and hateful, he tells how they will
become ugly and crippled.*[11]

The Truth of the Cause of Suffering pinpoints the root problem of
suffering: ignorance. Because of ignorance we mistake our "self"
to be something that is born and dies. Confused about this
fundamental issue, we easily become driven by fear of death and
grasping at life, and thus we create infinite kinds of karma. In
reality our true nature was never born and will never perish. The
"self" that undergoes birth and death is an illusion, a phantasm of
our mind's making born of ignorance.

*Then the World Honored One explained the insubstantiality
of the self.
'Whatsoever is originated will be dissolved again. All
worry about the self is vain; the self is like a mirage,
and all the tribulations that touch it will pass away. They
will vanish like a nightmare when the sleeper awakes.*

*He who has Awakened is freed from fear; he has become
a Buddha; he knows the vanity of all his cares, his
ambitions, and also of his pains.*

*It easily happens that a man, when taking a bath, steps
upon a wet rope and imagines that it is a snake. Horror
will overcome him, and he will shake from fear,
anticipating in his mind all the agonies caused by the
serpent's venomous bite. What a relief does this man
experience when he sees that the rope is no snake. The
cause of his fright lies in his error, his ignorance, and*

his illusion. If the true nature of the rope is recognized, his peace of mind will come back to him; he will feel relieved; he will be joyful and happy.

This is the state of mind of one who has recognized that there is no self, that the cause of all his troubles, cares, and vanities is a mirage, a shadow, a dream.[12]

The Buddha used another analogy to describe how ignorance by nature has no cause, no reason for being. Indeed, the greatest mystery in life is "Why is there ignorance?" The Buddha said that we are like Yajnadatta, an Indian contemporary of the Buddha. One day Yajnadatta looked in a mirror and fell in love with his reflection. For no reason, he thought the head in the mirror belonged to someone else; that he did not have a head of his own. He suddenly went insane, and ran about madly screaming, "Where is my head! Where is my head!"

The Buddha said, "Was there any reason why he became fearful for his head and ran madly about? If his madness were to suddenly cease, it would not be because he "recovered" his head from someplace outside. So even before his madness ceased, how could his head have been lost?...."

"When the madness of the Yajnadatta in your own mind ceases, just that ceasing is Enlightenment. The supreme, pure, bright mind originally pervades all reality. It is not something obtained from anyone else.[13]*"*

With your own mind, you grasp at your own mind.
What is not illusory turns into illusion.
If you don't grasp, there is no non-illusion.
If even non-illusion does not arise,

19

How can illusory dharmas be established?
This is called the wondrous lotus flower,
the regal vajra gem of Enlightenment.[14]

[1]*Rulers of the World,* Chapter 1, *Flower Adornment Sutra.* "Afflictions" is a translation of the Sanskrit *kleshas* which literally means "causing pain, distress, or anguish."

[2]*Turning the Dharma Wheel Sutra, Dhamma Cakka Ppavattana Sutra, Samyutta Nikaya* LVI, 11.

[3]*Shurangama Sutra,* Volume 2, BTTS.

[4]*Shurangama Sutra,* Volume 1, BTTS.

[5]*Dharmapada, Verse 71.*

[6]*Flower Store Sea of Worlds,* Chapter 5, Volume 2, *Flower Adornment Sutra,* BTTS.

[7]*Sutra on Cause and Effect in the Three Periods of Time.* Complete text appears in *Filiality: the Human Source,* Volume 1, BTTS.

[8]ibid.

[9]ibid.

[10]ibid.

[11]*Sutra of the Past Vows of Earth Store Bodhisattva,* BTTS.

[12]*Pali Canon Sutras.*

[13]*Shurangama Sutra,* Volume 4. BTTS.

[14]ibid.

20

The Bodhisattva Manjushri, Foremost in Wisdom

Chapter Three

The Path to the Cessation of Suffering: Practicing the Dharma

Third Magnificent Vow of the Bodhisattva:
I vow to learn the measureless Dharma-doors.

Using measureless dharma-doors, he's totally free and easy.
He tames and regulates living beings
throughout the ten directions,
And yet while doing all of this among living beings,
the Bodhisattva is detached and makes no discriminations.[1]

This corresponds to the Noble Truth of the Path That Leads to the Cessation of Suffering.

> *What, Bhikshus, is the Noble Truth of the Path That Leads to the Cessation of Suffering? Just this eightfold path; namely right views, right intention, right speech, right behavior, right livelihood, right effort, right mindfulness, and right meditative-concentration.*[2] (The Bodhisattva's Dharma-doors or methods of practice are the Six Perfections: giving, morality, patience, vigor, meditative-concentration and wisdom.) The Path should be practiced.

The word Dharma refers to the Buddha's teachings. As mentioned before it literally refers to the laws or truths that govern reality. In Buddhism it particularly alludes to the methods of practice the Buddha compassionately set forth to guide living beings through the dense forest of their ignorance to the light of their true nature.

The Dharma offers a profound analysis of the problem of suffering, while providing both an alternate vision free of suffering (Enlightenment) and the actual methods we need to realize that awakening.

Simply put, the Dharma is:

Not doing any evil.
Reverently practicing all good.
Purifying one's own mind.
That is the teaching of all Buddhas.[3]

The essential Dharmas of practice consist of morality, meditative-concentration, and wisdom.

From the moral precepts comes meditative-concentration,
and out of meditative-concentration arises wisdom.[4]

Morality

Without a strong foundation in moral conduct it is impossible to develop skill in meditation and to acquire the genuine meditative-concentration that leads to wisdom. The Buddha established the Five Moral Precepts as basic virtues for human life and the very essence of spiritual cultivation. They are as follows:

1. *Do not kill.* We should not deliberately kill any living creature, either by committing the act ourselves, instructing others to kill, participating in or approving of acts of killing. One can avoid indirect involvement in killing by eating only vegetarian food. Compassion, mutual respect for life, and a sense of oneness with all living creatures are compelling reasons for holding this precept.

2. *Do not steal.* If something is not given to us, we should not

take it. This precept applies not only to valuable items such as gold and silver, but even to things as small and inexpensive as needles. This can also be interpreted as living frugally and not wasting resources.

3. *Do not engage in sexual misconduct.* Sexual activities with anyone other than our lawful spouse are considered promiscuous. Promiscuous sex, or perverse sex, such as homosexuality and sexual activity with animals, leads to rebirth in the lower realms of existence in which one experiences much suffering.

4. *Do not speak falsely.* In general, there are four kinds of incorrect   speech: lying, irresponsible speech, (such as gossip and talk which upsets people's emotions); abusive speech, (such as harshly berating others); and backbiting speech (which causes dissension and discord among people).

5. *Do not take intoxicants.* Alcohol, illicit drugs, stimulants, or depressants and even tobacco are all considered intoxicants. They harm the body, confuse our spirit, and cause us to be dull-witted in future lives.

> *Now I will describe the rules of conduct a householder should follow to become a good disciple. However, if one wishes to fulfill the duties of a Bhikshu, one cannot do so by possessing the property of a householder.*

> *Let him not destroy life nor cause others to destroy life, nor approve of others' killing. Let him refrain from oppressing all living beings in the world, whether strong or weak.*

25

Then because the disciple knows that it belongs to others, stealing anything from any place should be avoided. Let him neither steal, nor approve of others' stealing. All stealing should be avoided.

The wise man should avoid a non-celibate life as he would a burning charcoal pit. If he is unable to lead a celibate life fully, let him not transgress with another's wife.

Whether in an assembly or in a public place let him not lie to another. Let him neither cause others to lie nor approve of others' telling lies.

The householder who delights in self-control, knowing that intoxicants destroy it, neither takes intoxicants, nor would he lead others to take them, nor approve of others' doing so.[5]

Moral precepts are the foundation for Enlightenment.[6]

The moral precepts of Buddhism are rooted in self-respect (especially cherishing one's spiritual nature) and respect for others. Self-respect and respect for others in turn develop naturally out of our first and most fundamental human relationship: child and parents. Kindness, compassion, generosity and mercy as well as our self-esteem are all kindled and instilled within the ongoing give and take of that relationship. Thus in the discourse on the Bodhisattva Precepts from the *Brahma Net Sutra* the Buddha observes that:

Filial compliance is a dharma of the ultimate path. Filiality is known as moral precepts. It is also called restraint and stopping.

The most basic human virtue is reverence for one's father and mother. The Buddha regarded filial piety as absolutely essential to a moral life.

Bhikshus, there are two persons whom you can never repay. They are your mother and father. Even if you were to carry your mother on one shoulder and your father on the other for one hundred years, and they should even void their excrement there; and if you should attend to them, anointing them with salves, massaging, bathing and rubbing their limbs, even that would not repay them.

Even if you were to establish your parents as the supreme lords and rulers over this earth, rich in the seven treasures (gold, silver, lapis lazuli, crystal, red pearls, mother of pearls and carnelian), this still would not be a sufficient display of gratitude. Why? Parents do so much for their children, Bhikshus. They bring them up, feed them, and guide them through this world.[7]

And in the following passage from the *Sutra of the Deep Kindness of Parents and the Difficulty of Repaying It*, the Buddha poignantly describes what parents do for their children.[8]

For ten (lunar) months while the mother carries the child, she feels discomfort each time she rises, as if she were lifting a heavy burden. Like a chronic invalid, she is unable to keep down her food and drink. When the ten months have passed and the time comes for giving birth, she undergoes much pain and suffering so that the child can be born. She fears for her own life, like a pig or lamb waiting to be slaughtered. Then the blood flows all over the ground. These are the sufferings she undergoes.

27

Once the child is born, she saves the sweet for it and swallows the bitter herself. She carries the child and nourishes it, washing away its filth. There is no toil or difficulty she does not willingly undertake for the sake of her child. She endures both cold and heat and never even mentions what she has gone through. She gives the dry place to her child and sleeps in the damp herself. For three years she nourishes the baby with milk, transformed from the blood of her own body.

Parents continually instruct and guide their children in the ways of propriety and morality as the youngsters mature into adults. They arrange marriages for them and provide them with property and wealth or sound advice on how to obtain these things. They take this responsibility and trouble upon themselves with tremendous zeal and toil, never mentioning their toil and kindness.

When a son or daughter becomes ill, parents are so worried and afraid that they may even grow ill themselves. They remain by the child's side providing constant care, and only when the child gets well are the parents happy once again. In this way, they cherish and raise their children with the sustained hope that their offspring will soon grow to be mature adults.

From this we begin to appreciate the deep debt of kindness we owe our parents. In this same Sutra the Buddha suggested some ways we can show our gratitude:

Disciples of the Buddha, if you wish to repay your parents' kindness, write out this Sutra on their behalf.

Recite this Sutra on their behalf. Repent of transgressions and offenses on their behalf. For the sake of your parents, make offerings to the Triple Jewel (the Buddha, the Dharma and the Sangha). For the sake of your parents, hold the precept of pure eating (vegetarian eating). For the sake of your parents, practice giving and cultivate blessings. If you are able to do these things, you are being a filial child.[9]

In the *Sigalaka Sutra*[10] the Buddha advised the layman *Sigalaka* how to live a wholesome and happy life. The Buddha outlined the respective duties and responsibilities one owes to father and mother, teachers, wife and children, friends, workers, and the religious. The following is advice on good friends and the management of personal wealth.

The friend who is a helper and the friend through thick and thin; the friend who shows the way that's proper and the friend full of sympathy: a wise person knows the true worth of these four kinds of friends and cherishes them with care, as a mother her dearest child.

The wise one trained and disciplined shines like a beacon; he gathers wealth just as the bee gathers honey, or ants build their mound. With wealth so gained, a layperson can devote it to people's good. One should divide one's wealth into four parts. One part may be enjoyed at will. Two parts should be put to work and the fourth part should be set aside as a reserve in times of need.

Whether one is a layperson or a monk or nun, morality constitutes the essential foundation for any genuine spiritual understanding

29

and experience. Although the specific precepts (the "letter") vary slightly between monastics and the laity, between monks and nuns, the underlying goal and rationale (the "spirit") is the same: to foster the virtuous qualities that develop concentration and allow wisdom to unfold.

Meditative-concentration

By upholding the moral prohibitions we purify the activities of body and speech, thereby laying a firm foundation for transforming the more deeply rooted and subtle habits of the mind. Meditation develops concentration. This in turn enhances our innate clarity of mind allowing us to see through the transient and superficial to the heart of things. As a result of this insight we become less flustered by trivial matters, more impervious to life's little ups and downs. A pleasant sense of calm and dispassion gradually ensues enabling one to experience less and less suffering because of the effect of external events. The methods for developing concentration vary: sitting in meditation, as well as forms of standing and walking meditation; reciting the names of the Buddhas or Bodhisattvas, bowing to the Buddhas or Bodhisattvas, bowing repentances, bowing to the Sutras, reciting the Sutras, and reciting mantras.[11] The possibilities are actually limitless; different methods suited to different people at different times. Although the methods vary, if practiced with utter absorption and underpinned with virtue, the result is the same: wisdom.

The following passage from the *Shurangama Sutra, Volume 8,* describes what occurs when we enter the initial stages of meditative-concentration.

> *Ananda, be aware that as you sit in the Bodhimanda (a place, such as a monastery, where the Dharma is*

practiced), you are doing away with all thoughts. When those thoughts come to an end you are free of all thinking. You enter a state of unadulterated clarity. Your mind no longer shifts between movement and stillness, and remembering and forgetting become one and the same.

When you dwell in this place and enter samadhi, you are like a person with vision who lives in utter darkness. The wonderfully pure mind that is your pristine nature does not yet emit light. This is called the "region of the form skandha." If the person's eyes become clear, then he experiences the ten directions as an open expanse and the darkness[12] is gone.

Wisdom (Prajna)

In Buddhism, there are three kinds of wisdom or prajna[13]: literary wisdom, which arises from the study of the Sutras, contemplative wisdom, by which one deeply ponders the meaning of the Sutras and then attains true understanding, and the wisdom of reality, by which one sees the true nature of reality. All phenomena in the universe have their own characteristics, yet ultimately they are mere conditioned appearances having no substantial nature of their own. That is, every phenomenon is analogous to a flower. A flower begins to arise after a seed is planted in the earth. When the seed receives water and sunlight in a timely manner, it will eventually blossom into a flower. The existence of the flower depends on all of these supporting conditions of the earth, water, and sunlight, as well as the basic cause of the seed. The flower does not have any inherent or independent being apart from these supporting conditions. When one sees that all things are like this,

31

then one has the revelation that the true nature of reality is empty, i.e., beyond appearances. It is beyond the duality of existence and non-existence. Therefore, the wisdom of reality is a profound world — transcending insight into the real nature of all things. It sees the insubstantial nature of all phenomena and the true reality beyond appearances. This state cannot be conceptualized or described; it can only be known by actually experiencing it.

> *Contemplate the fundamental falseness of appearances. They are just like flowers conjured up in space that bear empty fruit. Why, then, investigate the meaning of their formation and disappearance?*[14]

Prajna empowers the Bodhisattvas who appear in the world over and over again to help living beings. Although they see that the true nature of reality is very profound, pure and perfect in itself, yet they appear in the illusory world — the distorted, misperceived reality, which living beings have created through their ignorance — in order to help all beings. Without this wisdom, they would be swept away with the current like everyone else. Wisdom, however, allows them to "enter the fire and not be burned." It enables them to be like the lotus flower rooted in the muck and mire but whose petals never touch the polluted water. Thus the Bodhisattvas embody the Dharma that they teach, and this embodiment of virtue, concentration, and wisdom is the true "speaking of Dharma." The teaching and the teacher become one and the same.

In teaching the Dharma, a Bodhisattva understands the limitless differences among living beings that stem from their past karma and present circumstances. To be effective, his teaching of the Dharma must be appropriate to their natures. Therefore, over the course of many lifetimes, he purposely traverses the paths of rebirth, studying the Dharma from many Buddhas and other

Bodhisattvas, learning the measureless methods for teaching and influencing the almost infinite number of sentient beings. In this way he acquires the ability to give the highest gift, the gift of the Dharma, to all living creatures.

Among all offerings, the offering of the Dharma is supreme. This is the offering of cultivating according to the teachings, the offering of gathering in living beings, the offering of benefiting living beings, the offering of standing in for living beings who are undergoing suffering, the offering of diligently cultivating the roots of good, the offering of not renouncing the karma of the Bodhisattvas, and the offering of never forsaking the Bodhi-mind.[15]

Excerpt from the *Vajra Prajna-Paramita Sutra*[16]
and explanation by Venerable Tripitaka Master
Hsuan Hua

All conditioned dharmas
Are like dreams, illusions, bubbles, shadows,
Like dew drops and a lightning flash:
Contemplate them thus.

Explanation of the Sutra: Everything is a *conditioned dharma*. Eating, wearing clothes, walking, standing, sitting, lying down, running a business — all activities are conditioned dharmas. These are examples of external conditioned dharmas. There are also the five constituents of existence: physical form, feeling, thought, volitional formation and consciousness which are conditioned dharmas. The four elements, that is earth (solids), water (liquids), fire (temperature), and air (motion) are conditioned dharmas. The six sense faculties, their objects, and the respective consciousness

33

that arises at each sense faculty when it is in contact with its object are all conditioned dharmas. All those dharmas whether external or internal, *Are like dreams, illusions, bubbles, shadows.*

What is a *dream*? No one knows. If we knew then we would not dream. People are in a perpetual dream. When you fall asleep and dream, you are unaware of the things which exist in your ordinary waking state, and when you awaken from the dream, you usually cannot remember the events of the dream. In the same way, we are unable to remember the events of our former lives, because they have disappeared in this present life's dream.

Someone may have a dream in which he becomes wealthy, is appointed an official, and is on the verge of becoming president, when suddenly someone else says to him, "Sir, you are actually having a dream." But in the midst of his dream of power and wealth, the person cannot believe what he is told.

"Everything that is happening to me is real," he says, "I'm wealthy, I'm an official, I'm a candidate for president. How can you say that I am dreaming?" However, when he awakens from his dream, without being told he will know that all those events happened in a dream.

So too we people are as if in a dream. Now I will tell you: this is a dream. Although I've told you, surely you will reply, "What do you mean, a dream? This is all real. These things are actually happening. How can you say it is a dream? You're just deceiving us."

When your spiritual cultivation is accomplished, without being told, you will awaken from this dream and know that everything you did in the past was a dream. The reason you do not believe me when I tell you that you are dreaming is that you still have not awakened from your dream. When you awaken you will agree, "Yes, it was all a dream."

Illusions are unreal, like a magician's tricks. The magician recites a mantra and a lotus flower suddenly appears in the water, or in the midst of fire. Or he may cause a piece of jade suddenly to appear as if from nowhere. A magician appears to have spiritual powers and miraculous abilities, but what he does is unreal. Although it seems real, if you investigate, it is seen to be illusory and non-existent. Children may be fooled into believing that the lotus in the fire is real, but an adult will take one look and know that it is a trick.

When you understand the Buddha-dharma you know that everything is empty and illusory. The world is empty and illusory; it comes into being from a conflux of conditions which only seem to be real. When you do not understand the Buddha-dharma, you are like the foolish child who considers everything to be real. This is not to belittle people: it is a simple fact. People who do not understand the Buddha-dharma think that being wealthy and having an official position are real. In actuality everything is one. Everything is the same. A person is the same whether he is rich or poor. If you understand that everything is empty and illusory, then you cannot be confused by anything. You will not become attached to unreal states.

Bubbles are also unreal, and quickly disappear, thereby revealing their emptiness.

Shadows follow people around. When there is form, then there is a shadow. The form has actual substance, but the shadow is empty. If explained in more depth, even form itself is empty and unreal. If you do not believe this, then just continue to cling to your body;

protect and maintain it, and see whether or not it dies.

Like dew drops and a lightning flash. If you look outside early in the morning you will find dew, but after sunrise the dew will have evaporated. A lightning flash is also quite evanescent.

Contemplate them thus. You should look upon all conditioned things in this way. If you do, then heaven will be empty and earth will be void. The measure of your mind will be as vast as the heavens and as broad as the reaches of space, free of any impediments. Without impediments you will have no fear whatsoever.

[1]*Rulers of the World*, Chapter 1, *Flower Adornment Sutra*.

[2]*Turning the Dharma Wheel Sutra (Dhamma Cakka Ppavattana Sutra)*, *Samyutta Nikaya* LVI, 11.

[3]*Dharmapada*, Verse 183.

[4]*Shurangama Sutra*, Volume 6, BTTS.

[5]Sutta-Nipata, II, 14, *Dhammika Sutra*. The text is a slightly modified version of a translation done by Venerable H. Saddhatissa, published as *The Sutta-Nipata* (1985, Curzon Press Ltd., London, England).

[6]*Bodhisattvas Ask for Clarification*, Chapter 10, *Flower Adornment Sutra*.

[7]*Anguttara Nikaya*, II, iv, 2.

[8]Complete text of *Sutra of The Deep Kindness of Parents and the Difficulty in Repaying It* appears in *Filiality: the Human Source*, Volume Two, BTTS.

[9]ibid.

[10]*Digha-Nikaya, Sutra 31*. The text is based on the translation by Maurice Walshe published as *Thus I Have Heard* (1987, Wisdom Publications, London, England).

[11]Refer to Chapters 6, 7 and 8 for detailed instructions about meditation.

[12]"*Skandha*" literally means "aggregate" or "bundle", it refers to the five constituents of existence mentioned in Chapter 1: physical form, feelings, thoughts, volitional formations, and consciousness.

[13]*Prajna* is a Sanskrit term which is not translated because it has many meanings, and also out of veneration.

[14]*Shurangama Sutra*, Volume 4, BTTS.

[15] *Universal Worthy's Conduct And Vows*, Chapter 40, *Flower Adornment Sutra*, BTTS.

[16] *Vajra Prajna-Paramita Sutra*, BTTS. "*Vajra*" is an indestructible substance. "*Paramita*", literally "arrived at the other shore", means to completely perfect whatever one does.

The Buddha Shakyamuni
of our World System

Chapter Four

The Cessation of Suffering: The Realm of the Buddha

Fourth Magnificent Vow of the Bodhisattva:
I vow to realize the unsurpassed path of the Buddha.

*The Thus Come One observes the world
and produces a heart of great compassion.
In order to benefit living beings, he appears
And shows them the peace and
happiness of the most supreme Path.*[1]

This corresponds to the Noble Truth of the Cessation of Suffering.

What, Bhikshus, is the Noble Truth of the Cessation of Suffering? It is the passionless cessation of this very thirst (mentioned in the Truth of the Cause of Suffering) without remainder. Abandoning and renouncing it, being released from and averting from it.[2] The Cessation of Suffering should be realized.

The Bodhisattva perfects his Enlightenment through study and practice over many lifetimes. The Bodhisattva then becomes a Buddha. "Buddha" literally means "Awakened One" or "Enlightened One". He is one of ultimate wisdom and compassion. His wisdom encompasses the entire universe without obstruction; his compassion for beings in all states of existence in all worlds knows no bounds. Only when one becomes a Buddha, will one fully realize the cessation of all suffering.

Therefore, the realm of the Buddha is difficult to fathom. Those who see the Buddha perceive him differently reflecting their own karma. For example, the great Bodhisattvas observe the Buddha always teaching and influencing living beings in every realm of existence. In contrast, common people, because of their limited knowledge and vision, find it difficult to even believe or imagine the state of a Buddha.

How can living beings in the three realms of existence, in their worldly state and even the Sound Hearers and Those Enlightened to Conditions[3] in their transcendent state, speculate about the Supreme Enlightenment of the Thus Come One? With their limited minds and worldly language and expressions, how could they enter the knowledge and vision of the Buddha?[4]

The wisdom of all the Buddhas is limitless and most profound. The gateway to this wisdom is difficult to discover, difficult to enter. It cannot by known by any of the Sound Hearers or Pratyeka Buddhas.[5]

Why? In the past, these Buddhas have drawn near to countless billions of Buddhas, exhaustively practicing their uncountable Dharmas of the Path.[6]

Only one Buddha comes into a world-system at a time, but many Buddhas *may* appear in a single world system in succession. After the previous Buddha's Dharma has totally disappeared from the world, the next Buddha appears prompting the Dharma to flourish again. For example, in the *Sutra of the Ultimate Extinction of the Dharma*, Shakyamuni Buddha discusses Maitreya Buddha, the next Buddha to appear in our world system.

When my Dharma disappears, it will be like an oil lamp

which flares brightly for an instant just before it goes out. So too, will the Dharma flare and die. It is difficult to speak with certainty of what will follow after that time.

And so it will remain for the next ten million years. Then, when Maitreya is about to appear in the world as the next Buddha, the planet will be entirely peaceful. Evil vapors will have dissipated, rain will be ample and regular, the crops will grow abundantly.[7]

Nor is there just *one* Buddha. In the Sutras the Buddha explained that numerous world systems in the universe have Buddhas in them.

Shariputra, all Buddhas, the World Honored Ones, throughout the ten directions in limitless quadrillions of Buddha-lands, presently are greatly benefiting living beings and bringing them peace and happiness.[8]

The following selection of Sutra passages describes the scope of the Buddha's compassion and wisdom.

The Buddha's Compassion

The Buddha contemplates all those in the world: upside-down, ever confused and deluded. They revolve in the suffering of birth and death; so he gives rise to a heart of great compassion. Throughout billions of eons, he cultivates the practices of Enlightenment, wishing to rescue beings through the power of great compassion.

His head, eyes, hands, feet and so forth, all he can totally renounce for the sake of seeking Enlightenment. He does this for limitless eons.[9]

41

The Buddha toiled through eons
for the sake of living beings,
Cultivating limitless, oceanic great compassion.
In order to comply with living beings
he enters birth and death,
Transforming the multitudes everywhere, and causing
them to be pure.[10]

The Buddha's Wisdom

All the gods and people in the world, and all species of
living beings, cannot know the Buddhas. The Buddhas'
powers, fearlessness, liberations and samadhis, and
other Dharmas of the Buddhas, cannot be fathomed by
anyone. Long ago, I followed countless Buddhas; I
perfectly walked all the paths of the Dharma, subtle,
wonderful and deep, hard to see and hard to grasp.
Through limitless millions of eons, I walked down all
these paths. In the place of Enlightenment, I realized
the fruit, and have fully known and seen everything.[11]

Knowing the conduct of living beings, the thoughts deep
within their minds, Their habitual actions in the past,
the nature of their desires, the power of their vigor, and
their faculties, keen or dull, they employ various past
causes, analogies and expressions, teaching them with
appropriate skill-in-means.[12]

Further seen are all the Buddhas, the Lions, the Sagely
Masters, expounding on the supreme subtlety and wonder
of the Sutras. Clear and pure is the sound of their gentle,
mild voices, teaching all the Bodhisattvas, numbering
in the countless millions. This pure sound, profound and

wondrous, fills those who hear it with joy, as within his world, each one proclaims the proper Dharma. Using past causes and limitless analogies, they clarify the Buddha-dharma to enlighten living beings.[13]

The Scope of the Buddha's Spiritual Power

The Buddha told the Bhikshus, "In the past, limitless, boundless, inconceivable, asamkhyeyas[14] *of eons ago, there was a Buddha named Vast Penetrating Wisdom Victory, Thus Come One, One Worthy of Offerings, One of Proper and Universal Knowledge, One Whose Understanding and Conduct are Complete, Well Gone One Who Understands the World, Unsurpassed Lord, Taming and Regulating Hero, Teacher of Gods and Humans, Buddha, World Honored One. His country was named 'Good City', and his eon was named 'Great Mark'. O Bhikshus, it has been a great, long time since that Buddha passed into Nirvana."*

"Now suppose someone were to grind all the earths in a galaxy of a billion world systems into ink powder. Then suppose he traveled beyond a thousand worlds to the east and dropped a particle of that ink powder the size of a mote of dust. Then passing through another thousand worlds he deposited another mote, and continued to do this until all the ink supply made from these earths was exhausted."

"What do you think? Could a mathematician or his students ever finish computing those worlds and know their number?"

"No, World Honored One."

"O Bhikshus, if the lands this person had passed through, whether or not he set down a particle in them, were all ground into dust, and if each dust mote was equal to an eon, then the time since that Buddha passed into Nirvana would exceed that number by limitless, boundless, quadrillions of asamkhyeyas of eons."

"The power of the Thus Come One's knowledge and vision lets me behold that time in the distant past as if it were today."[15]

All Buddhas share the same special characteristics and qualities unique to a Buddha. The following are lists of some of the most well-known attributes and virtues of a Thus Come One.

The Ten Powers of a Buddha

1. The wisdom-power of being enlightened to what is possible or not possible.
2. The wisdom-power of knowing the karmic retributions in the past, present and future.
3. The wisdom-power of knowing all of the dhyanas[16], liberations, and samadhis.
4. The wisdom-power of knowing the superiority or inferiority of the faculties of all living beings.
5. The wisdom-power of knowing all of the various understandings of living beings.
6. The wisdom-power of knowing all of the various realms of living beings.
7. The wisdom-power of knowing where all paths lead.
8. The wisdom-power of the knowledge derived from the

44

unobstructed Heavenly Eye.

9. The wisdom-power, free from outflows, of knowing former lives.

10. The wisdom power of having severed all habitual energies forever.

The Eighteen Exceptional Characteristics of a Buddha

1. His body is flawless.
2. His speech is flawless.
3. His thought is flawless.
4. He has no perception of differences.
5. He has no unconcentrated thoughts.
6. There is nothing he does not know and has not already renounced.
7. His resolve never diminishes.
8. His vigor never diminishes.
9. His mindfulness never wanes.
10. His wisdom never wanes.
11. His liberation never diminishes.
12. His knowledge and vision of liberation never diminish.
13. All of his bodily karma is done with wisdom.
14. All of his speech karma is done with wisdom.
15. All of his thought karma is done with wisdom
16. His wisdom gives him unobstructed knowledge of the past.
17. His wisdom gives him unobstructed knowledge of the future.
18. His wisdom gives him unobstructed knowledge of the present.

The Thirty-two Physical Hallmarks of a Buddha

1. Level and full feet.
2. Thousand-spoke wheels on each of his feet.

3. Long, slender fingers.

4. Supple and soft hands and feet.

5. Fine webbing lacing his fingers and toes.

6. Well set and even heels.

7. Arched insteps.

8. Thighs like the royal stag Aineya (king of deer).

9. Long, graceful hands which reach below the knees.

10. Well-retracted male organ (like that of a horse).

11. Height and stretch of arms equal.

12. Every hair root imperial blue color.

13. Hair on his body curling upward.

14. Body the color of true gold.

15. Ten foot aura encircling him.

16. Soft, smooth skin.

17. The seven places (the convex places at the back of the four limbs, the two shoulders and the trunk of the body) distinctive and full.

18. Well filled area below the armpits.

19. Upper torso like that of a royal lion.

20. Body erect and upright.

21. Full and round shoulders like a Nyagrodha tree (perfectly symmetrical like the Banyan tree).

22. Forty teeth.

23. Teeth white, even and close.

24. Four pure white canine teeth.

25. Jaws like a lion.

26. Saliva which improves the taste of all food.

27. Vast and long tongue.

28. Voice deep and resonant (emits Brahma-pure sounds).

29. Eyes violet blue.

30. Eyelashes like a royal bull.

31. White hair-tuft (urna) between the eyebrows which emits light.
32. Cowl on the summit of his crown.
    Each of these attributes is a natural reward for a specific kind of good karma Buddhas create during many past lives.

The Ten Titles of a Buddha

1. Thus Come One.
2. One Worthy of Offerings.
3. One of Proper and Universal Knowledge.
4. One Perfect in Understanding and Conduct.
5. Well Gone One Who Understands the World.
6. Unsurpassed Lord.
7. Hero Who Tames and Regulates.
8. Teacher of Gods and Humans.
9. Buddha.
10. World Honored One.

[1]*Rulers of the World*, Chapter 1, *Flower Adornment Sutra*.
[2]*Turning the Dharma Wheel Sutra, Dhamma Cakka Ppavattana Sutra, Samyutta Nikaya* LVI, 11.
[3]"Sound Hearers", also known as "Arhats", are Sages who have attained a level of genuine Enlightenment in the Buddha's teaching. "Those Enlightened to Conditions", and "Pratyeka Buddhas", like the Arhats, are enlightened Sages. Refer to the section on the "Sangha of the Sages" in Chapter 5.
[4]*Shurangama Sutra*, Volume 4, BTTS.
[5]Pratyeka Buddha literally means a "Solitary Buddha". This is an individual who like the Arhat on the 4th Stage (see Chapter 5, "Sangha of the Sages") has attained personal liberation, that is, he has transcended the realm of Samsara. Unlike the Arhat, he has discovered the path to Enlightenment on his own like a Buddha has done. However, he does not have the ability to teach living beings in the way a Buddha does.
[6]*Expedient Devices*, Chapter 2, *Dharma Flower Sutra*, Volume 3, BTTS.
[7]The complete text of this Sutra appears in the Preface to the *Shurangama*

Sutra, Volume 1, BTTS.

[8]*Expedient Devices*, Chapter 2, *Dharma Flower Sutra*, Volume 3, BTTS.

[9]*Entering the Dharma Realm*, Chapter 39, Part 5, *Flower Adornment Sutra*.

[10]*Wondrous Adornments of the World-Rulers*, Chapter 1, *Flower Adornment Sutra*.

[11]*Expedient Devices*, Chapter 2, *Dharma Flower Sutra*, Volume 3, BTTS.

[12]*Expedient Devices*, Chapter 2, *Dharma Flower Sutra*, Volume 3, BTTS.

[13]*Introduction*, Chapter 1, *Dharma Flower Sutra*, Volume 2, BTTS.

[14]"*Asamkhyeya*" means an immeasurable number.

[15]*Transformation City*, Chapter 7, *Dharma Flower Sutra*, Volume 7, BTTS.

[16]"*Dhyana*" literally means meditation or absorption in abstract thought. Refer to Appendix I, Chart of *Samsara*, the Realm of Birth and Death.

Review of the Four Noble Truths and the Bodhisattva's Four Magnificent Vows

First Magnificent Vow of the Bodhisattva:
I vow to rescue the boundless living beings from suffering.

The Buddha toils through eons for the sake of living beings
Cultivating limitless, oceanic, great compassion.
To comply with living beings, he enters birth and death,
Transforming the multitudes everywhere,
so they become pure.[1]

This vow corresponds to *the Noble Truth of Suffering.*

What, Bhikshus, is the Noble Truth of Suffering? Birth is suffering; old age is suffering; sickness is suffering; death is suffering; sorrow, lamentation, pain, grief, and despair are suffering; to be together with what or those you hate is suffering; to be separated from what or those you love is suffering; not to obtain what you wish for is suffering; in general, identification with the Five Constituents of Existence (physical form, feelings, thoughts, volitional formations, and consciousness) is suffering.[2] The Truth of Suffering should be understood.

Second Magnificent Vow of the Bodhisattva:
I vow to put an end to the infinite afflictions of living beings.

Living beings are drowning in the sea of afflictions.

Defiled by deluded and confused views,
they are quite alarming.
The Great Teacher feels pity in his heart and enables
them to separate from afflictions forever.[3]

This corresponds to *the Noble Truth of the Cause of Suffering.*

What, Bhikshus, is the Noble Truth of the Cause of Suffering? Just this thirst, leading to being, accompanied by delight and passion, gratifying itself now here and now there; namely the thirst for sense pleasures, the thirst for being, and the thirst for non-being.[4] (This "thirst" implies ignorance of the first truth of suffering. Ignorance and thirst are the most fundamental afflictions.) The Cause of Suffering should be cut off.

Third Magnificent Vow of the Bodhisattva:
I vow to learn the measureless Dharma-doors.

Using measureless dharma-doors, he's totally free and easy.
He tames and regulates living beings
throughout the ten directions,
And yet while doing all of this among living beings,
the Bodhisattva is detached and makes no discriminations.[5]

This corresponds to *the Noble Truth of the Path That Leads to the Cessation of Suffering.*

What, Bhikshus, is the Noble Truth of the Path That Leads to the Cessation of Suffering? Just this eightfold path; namely right views, right intention, right speech, right behavior, right livelihood, right effort, right mindfulness, and right meditative-concentration.[6] (The Bodhisattva's Dharma-doors or methods of practice are the Six Perfections:

giving, morality, patience, vigor, meditative concentration and wisdom.) The Path should be practiced.

Fourth Magnificent Vow of the Bodhisattva:
I vow to realize the unsurpassed path of the Buddha.

The Thus Come One observes the world
and produces a heart of great compassion.
In order to benefit living beings, he appears
And shows them the peace and happiness
of the most supreme Path.[7]

This corresponds to *the Noble Truth of the Cessation of Suffering.*

What, Bhikshus, is the Noble Truth of the Cessation of Suffering? It is the passionless cessation of this very thirst (mentioned in the Truth of the Cause of Suffering) without remainder. Abandoning and renouncing it, being released from and averting from it.[8] The Cessation of Suffering should be realized. Only when one becomes a Buddha, will one fully realize the cessation of all suffering.

[1]*Rulers of the World*, Chapter 1, *Flower Adornment Sutra.*

[2]*Turning the Dharma Wheel Sutra, Dhamma Cakka Ppavattana Sutra, Samyutta Nikaya* LVI, 11.

[3]*Rulers of the World*, Chapter 1, *Flower Adornment Sutra.* "Afflictions" is a translation of the Sanskrit *kleshas* which literally means "causing pain, distress, or anguish."

[4]*Turning the Dharma Wheel Sutra, Dhamma Cakka Ppavattana Sutra, Samyutta Nikaya* LVI, 11.

[5]*Rulers of the World*, Chapter 1, *Flower Adornment Sutra.*

[6]*Turning the Dharma Wheel Sutra (Dhamma Cakka Ppavattana Sutra), Samyutta Nikaya* LVI, 11.

[7]*Rulers of the World*, Chapter 1, *Flower Adornment Sutra.*

[8]*Turning the Dharma Wheel Sutra, Dhamma Cakka Ppavattana Sutra, Samyutta Nikaya* LVI, 11.

The Bodhisattva Earth Treasury
(Kshitigarbha),
Foremost in Vows

Chapter Five

Sangha, the Third Jewel

*All sentient beings, if they seek the Unsurpassed, Proper
and Equal, Right Enlightenment and the happiness of
Nirvana, must take refuge with the Triple Jewel.*[1]

People who believe in the Buddha's teachings should formally
take refuge with the Triple Jewel. The Triple Jewel is the Buddha,
the Dharma, and the Sangha. The third of the three jewels, the
Sangha, literally means "harmoniously united assembly." In the
Six Paramitas Sutra the Buddha noted three kinds of Sangha.

*The first is the Sangha of the Primary Meaning, consisting
of the Sagely Sangha of Buddhas who abide by the
Dharma. The second is the Sangha of the Sages. The
third is the 'field of blessings Sangha', comprised of the
Bhikshus and Bhikshunis who receive and uphold the
moral precepts.*

The Sangha of the Buddhas consists of all the infinite numbers of
Buddhas in the world-systems of the universe. In the Buddhist
world, however, the word Sangha generally refers to the Bhikshu
and Bhikshuni Sangha — the lowest of the three types mentioned
by the Buddha. The use of the word "sangha" to refer to the
common lay community is misleading and a departure from the
traditional usage and meaning of the word, as will be explained
later in this chapter.

The Sangha of Bhikshus and Bhikshunis

The "field of blessings Sangha" consists of Bhikshus and Bhikshunis — men and women who have left the householder's life and completed traditional ordination procedures in which they take vows to strictly adhere to the monastic code laid down by the Buddha. The core of this code of self-discipline (the Vinaya) is celibacy, not taking life, not stealing, and total honesty. The code also includes renunciation of wealth and shunning worldly entertainment. Members of the Bhikshu and Bhikshuni Sangha shave their heads (a symbol of casting off the mundane for the spiritual life) and wear traditional monastic robes that vary somewhat in color and design according to the climate and customs of their respective countries. Their clothing is simple and unadorned — its primary purpose to protect the wearer from the elements. It bears a distinctive cut, however, so as to clearly distinguish monks (Bhikshus) and nuns (Bhikshunis) from the laity, and thereby notify and remind the laity to treat the Sangha in a manner appropriate to their celibate way of life.

The importance of the Sangha is demonstrated in the life of the Buddha. As a young prince the Buddha experienced what are known as the "four signs". The first three signs of an old person, a sick person and a dead person were already described in Chapter One. What was the fourth sign? A Bhikshu.

At that time a god from the Pure Abodes,
Transfigured as a Bhikshu,
And appeared before the prince.
The prince respectfully stood and welcomed him. He asked, "Who are you ?"
The monk replied, "A Shramana (another term for a Bhikshu). Loathing old age, sickness and death I've left

the life of a householder to seek liberation. Old age, sickness, and death bring change and decay to living beings without a moment's rest. Therefore, I seek eternal happiness, which neither ceases nor begins. My mind looks equally upon enemy and friend. I care not for wealth and sex. I dwell in the mountain forests, in the quiet wilderness, without managing any affairs. My worldly thoughts have faded away. Alone I abide at ease in quietude. I don't choose between the fine and coarse. I beg to support my body." Then right before the prince's eyes, the monk deftly leapt into the sky and disappeared. The prince was delighted, and marveled at how the Buddhas of the past discovered and passed on this majestic way of life.[2]

After seeing this Bhikshu, the prince Siddhartha followed the same way of life. He renounced the life of a householder in quest of the solution to the problem of birth and death. When he made this resolve, his father, the king, as well as the king's ministers, tried to stop the young man by commanding his concubines to arouse the young prince's worldly passions.

There were those who held or hugged him, or arranged his pillow and bed, or lay next to him, saying sweet words, or teased him in a common worldly way, or spoke of many sexual activities, or tempted him with all manner of sexual acts to entice him from his resolve.

The Bodhisattva's mind was pure, solid and difficult to move. As he heard the harem women speak, he felt neither sadness nor joy, but grew in his feeling of disgust. He sighed, 'This is really strange. Now I know all these women's hearts are heavy with desire in this way, but

55

don't they realize that their young and robust forms will soon be ravaged by death and old age? How pitiful their great confusion. Delusion envelops their minds. They should be mindful of old age and death and day and night diligently urge themselves on. It's as if a sharp knife were poised at one's neck. How can one casually laugh? Seeing others grow old, turn sick and die, and not think to look at oneself is to be like a clay or wooden statue. How senseless!'[3]

The concubines could not dent the Prince's resolve. He renounced his royal position, wealth, and all things worldly for the drab garments and shorn head of a mendicant. With a light heart and iron resolve he set out on the ultimate spiritual journey: perfect enlightenment and deliverance from the "prison of the world."

After the Buddha's Enlightenment, some who heard his teaching wished to devote their entire lives to practicing it. Following the Buddha's example, they too renounced the householder's life, shaved their heads, and took up the monastic life under the Buddha.

The Buddha said, "Men are bound by their wives (and women by their husbands), children, and homes to such an extent that it is worse than being in prison. The time comes when you are released from prison, but there is never a moment when you think of leaving your wife and children. Don't you fear the control that emotion, love, and sex have over you? Although you are in a tiger's mouth, you are blissfully oblivious to it. Those who throw themselves in the mud and drown are known as ordinary people. By passing through this door and transcending defiling objects, you become a Sage."[4]

As to love and desire: no desire is as deep-rooted as sex. There is nothing stronger than the desire for sex. Fortunately, it is one of a kind. If there were something else like it, no one in the entire world would be able to cultivate the spiritual path.[5]

Be careful not to trust your own mind; your own mind cannot be trusted. Be careful not to get involved in sex; involvement with sex leads to disaster. Once you have become a Sage (Arhat) then you can trust your own mind.[6]

Bhikshus who have left the householder's life, turn back desire, give up love, and recognize the source of the mind. They penetrate the Buddha's profound principles, and awaken to the Unconditioned. They seek nothing outside; cling to nothing within.[7]

The Sangha is a field of blessings. The Bhikshus and Bhikshunis who receive and uphold the moral prohibitions are learned and wise. Like the trees created by the gods, they are able to protect living beings. To encounter the Sangha is like being drenched in a downpour of heavenly sweet rain when one is parched and thirsty in a barren desert. The rain is both timely and satisfying. Moreover, it is like the vast ocean — the source of manifold treasures.

The Sangha Jewel, as a field of blessings, is also like this. It can bestow peace and bliss upon all sentient beings. Moreover, this Sangha Jewel is pure and undefiled. It is able to dispel the darkness of living beings' greed, hatred and stupidity, like the bright light of the full moon that all beings gaze at with awe in the evening. It is also like a precious mani pearl that can fulfill all the good wishes of sentient beings.[8]

In the *Sutra of Changes to Come* the Buddha taught that the Dharma will disappear from the world simultaneously with the disappearance of the Sangha of Bhikshus and Bhikshunis, since the Dharma relies on the Sangha for its existence in the world.

The Sangha of the Sages

Above the Sangha of Bhikshus and Bhikshunis is yet a higher Sangha: the Sangha of the Sages. This includes those who have realized the Arhat or Bodhisattva levels of Enlightenment. The "Stream-enterer", lowest of the four stages of Arhats, is fundamentally different from ordinary people. The minds of common people continuously seek for pleasurable experiences outside through the sense organs. The Stream-enterer has turned his mind around, tending inwards, away from sense objects. This is a natural result of the unfolding of wisdom that has forever eliminated the "view of a self". That is, the Stream-enterer profoundly sees that there is nothing in *Samsara* that can be taken to be "I, mine, or my self". The Stream-enterer's position is irreversible: he can never be like a common person again, nor fall into the three lower realms of existence (animals, ghosts and beings in the hells). He is incapable of transgressing the Five Precepts. Within, at most, seven lives, he will become a fourth stage Arhat. For all of these reasons, he is said to have entered the stream of the Sages.

Making an offering of food to 10,000 people who hold the Five Precepts does not equal offering food to a single Stream-enterer.[9]

58

The fruit of the Stream-enterer surpasses kingship over the whole earth. It is preferable to rebirth in the heavens, and better than supreme rulership over all worlds.[10]

The Sage's experience of the world is difficult for common people to fathom. They acquire psychic abilities that coincide with their developed concentration and wisdom. They do not seek these abilities, sometimes called "spiritual penetrations", for even seeking spiritual power is contrary to the purpose of the Buddha's teachings. At the point of seeking nothing whatsoever, paradoxically, "one arrives," i.e., enlightenment occurs and one's innate wisdom and compassion come forth. This is the purport of the Buddha's method and instruction. So, while not an end in themselves, nonetheless spiritual penetrations can enable one to more effectively help other beings.

Fourth stage Arhats have ended birth and death in the three realms of existence. They possess the Five Eyes and the Six Spiritual Penetrations — highly developed psychic powers and extrasensory discernment.

The Five Eyes:

1. With the Heavenly Eye one can survey the different heavens and hells; one can see what the gods in the heavens are doing just as if watching a movie, and events thousands of miles away can be witnessed without impediment.

2. The Flesh Eye does not refer to the flesh eyes of ordinary people. Rather, it is a "spiritual eye" with which one can see spirits and ghosts.

3. With the Dharma Eye one observes relative truth. This eye enables one to understand all the affairs of worldly existence. It is said that with this eye one can see Buddhist Sutras in

every atomic particle.

4. The Wisdom Eye is the functioning of world-transcending wisdom (prajna). One comprehends the true nature of all phenomena as empty, i.e., without an intrinsic nature of their own, because all phenomena are relative and exist in dependence on other causes and conditions. Therefore, they have no inherent, real, or lasting independent existence.

5. With the Buddha Eye, the most powerful of the five spiritual eyes, analogous to a blazing sun, one can see billions of worlds systems without end.

The Six Spiritual Penetrations:

1. The Heavenly Eye. The same as the first of the Five Eyes above.

2. The Heavenly Ear can hear the speech and sounds of the gods in the heavens.

3. The Knowledge of Others' Thoughts. One knows the thoughts in others' minds before these thoughts are verbalized.

4. The Knowledge of Past Lives. One can know one's own and others' previous existences.

5. The Cessation of Outflows. One has extinguished greed, hatred, and stupidity forever, thereby transcending birth and death.

6. Spiritual Accomplishments. This refers to a host of minor spiritual powers.

People who are not Sages can acquire the Five Eyes and five of the Six Spiritual Penetrations. They cannot, however, obtain the penetration of the Cessation of Outflows. Only fourth stage Arhats gain that spiritual penetration. These "eyes" and penetrations come in many degrees and levels depending on the cultivated skill and karma of the individual. For example, a fourth stage Arhat can see the past lives of living beings as far back as 80,000 great kalpas — over a hundred quadrillion years, whereas a common person with the penetration of past lives may only be able to see back a few hundred years.

Moreover, even though the fourth and highest stage Arhats have ended birth and death in the three realms of existence of *Samsara* their enlightenment is not ultimate. A great achievement, nonetheless it is limited in scope, as it is only personal enlightenment.

The Bodhisattvas enlighten themselves and also enlighten other sentient beings. Their state of accomplishment is thus more difficult and more profound than the Arhats. The lowest level of Bodhisattva in the Sangha of the Sages is the "First Dwelling", called "One Who Has Brought Forth the Bodhi-Mind". *The Ten Dwellings*, Chapter 15 of the *Flower Adornment Sutra*, states that when a Bodhisattva attains this position, although he has not yet fully perfected the Ten Powers of a Buddha,[11] he enjoys ten kinds of wisdom which closely correspond to them. In *Entering the Dharma Realm*, Chapter 39 of the *Flower Adornment Sutra*, the pure youth Good Wealth visits a Bodhisattva on this level of Enlightenment. This Bodhisattva displays magnificent spiritual powers that enable him to visit Buddhas in millions of other worlds throughout the universe.

Indeed, in this chapter of the *Flower Adornment Sutra*, Good Wealth visits 55 Bodhisattvas, each of whom represents a successive level of Enlightenment. Some are human beings, some are gods, some are spirits. They appear in many shapes and forms as needed to help sentient beings. Their state, with its powers, compassion, and resourcefulness, is inconceivable. Therefore, the Sangha of the Sages can indeed appear as members of the laity. However, the common laity can by no means be considered to be members of the Sangha.

The realm of the Sangha of the Sages is very profound. One cannot claim such a level of attainment without certification by someone who is truly enlightened. Further, genuine Sages do not tell others that they are enlightened. They seek anonymity, not fame like common people. A person who tells people he is enlightened is actually very deluded. Thus, the Buddha forewarned that individuals openly proclaiming their "enlightenment" are merely deceiving themselves and deceiving others.

> *How can people who make such claims, other than at the end of their lives, and then only to those who inherit the teaching, be doing anything but deluding and confusing living beings and indulging in gross false claims?*[12]

Good and Wise Teachers

Members of the Sangha who are truly experienced cultivators of the Dharma, and those of the Sagely Sangha, are our good and wise teachers. For one practicing the Dharma it is absolutely essential, in order to make genuine progress, to secure the guidance of a good and wise teacher. Just as a child needs parents to protect, guide, and teach him while growing up, so too, in world-transcending matters, it is vital as a "child" in things spiritual to have a teacher to protect, guide and give instruction.

For example, as we progress in our Dharma practice and develop skill in meditation, we may experience some unusual states. These are all quite normal and often a sign of progress, although to the novice they may seem unusual and disconcerting. A good and wise teacher is familiar with these states and can interpret them, thus allaying any fears or equally deflating any pretensions of a beginner. Without mature and wise guidance, it is very easy to go down a wrong road. The closing volume of the *Shurangama Sutra* describes fifty states in particular which cultivators may experience and should be aware of.

Some inexperienced (and even experienced) meditators encounter these states and mistakenly think they have become enlightened. It is easy to see how a person without proper guidance could make this kind of critical error in judgment. The following is the first of the fifty states the Buddha describes in the *Shurangama Sutra*.

> *Ananda, be aware that as you sit in the Bodhimanda (a place, such as a monastery, where the Dharma is practiced), you are doing away with all thoughts. When those thoughts come to an end you are free of all thinking. You enter a state of unadulterated clarity. Your mind no longer shifts between movement and stillness, and remembering and forgetting become one and the same.*

> *When you dwell in this place and enter samadhi, you are like a person with clear vision who lives in utter darkness. The wonderfully pure mind that is your pristine nature does not yet emit light. This is called the region of the form skandha."*[13]

> *If the person's eyes become clear, then he experiences the ten directions as an open expanse and the darkness is gone. This is called, "the end of the form skandha." This person transcends the kalpa turbidity and can now contemplate its cause. This person can see that false notions of firmness and solidity form the basis of the form skandha.*

> *Ananda, at this point, when you are intently investigating*

that wondrous clarity, the four elements are no longer united, and soon the body can transcend obstructions. This is called "your essential light merging into the environment." It is a temporary state in the course of cultivation and does not indicate you're a Sage. If you do not think you have become a Sage, this could be a good state. But if you think you have become a Sage, you will make yourself vulnerable to the demons' influence.[14]

If we mistake any one of these states for an Enlightened state, we will certainly run spiritually aground. If, further, we then try to teach others, even if our intentions are pure, we will end up only confusing them as well and creating serious bad karma for ourselves. The importance of a genuine good and wise teacher becomes obvious when one studies the Sutras. His extensive personal experience and understanding of the Buddha's teachings has spelled, and will continue to spell, the difference between success and failure for students of the Dharma.

Good man, if you wish to accomplish All-wisdom, you must find a true, good and wise teacher. Good man, never tire of seeking for him, and upon encountering him, never grow weary of him. You must follow all of his teachings. And you must not find fault with his skill-in-means.[15]

Conclusion

Taking refuge with the Buddha, the Dharma, and the Sangha is the first step on the road to enlightenment and solving the problem of existence. "Why do I exist?" and "Who am I really?" These are questions all of us must grapple with and decide. They certainly deserve our very careful consideration. The unexamined life is a life lived in vain.

64

[1]*Six Paramitas Sutra.*
[2]*Acts of the Buddha (Buddhacharita)* by Master Ashvagosha.
[3]ibid.
[4]*Sutra in 42 Sections*, BTTS.
[5]ibid.
[6]ibid.
[7]ibid.
[8]*Six Paramitas Sutra.*
[9]*Sutra in 42 Sections*, BTTS.
[10]*Dharmapada.*
[11]See Chapter 4 for the complete list of the Ten Powers.
[12]*Shurangama Sutra.* Volume 6, BTTS.
[13]"*Skandha*" literally means "aggregate" or "bundle", it refers to the five constituents of existence mentioned in Chapter 1: physical form, feelings, thoughts, volitional formations, and consciousness.
[14]Refer to Appendix 1: A Chart of *Samsara* (the Realm of Birth and Death.)
[15]*Shurangama Sutra*, Volume 8. The importance of the *Shurangama Sutra* is verified by the Buddha when he says that it will be the first Sutra to disappear in our world when the Dharma begins to perish. Refer to the *Sutra of the Ultimate Extinction of the Dharma* which appears in the preface of *Shurangama Sutra*, Volume One, BTTS.

The Venerable Tripitaka
Master Hsuan Hua

Part II:

The Schools of Buddhist Practice

Below, by way of an introduction to this subject, is an interview with Venerable Tripitaka Master Hsuan Hua conducted by Karl Ray, which originally appeared in the former *Shambala Review* under the title *"Back to the Source"*

Karl Ray: (KR) The first question I would like to ask is based on an article in which you suggest that Buddhists forget sectarian lines. Can you suggest practical steps that Buddhist organizations can take to bring this about?

Master: (M) Before the Buddha came into the world there was no Buddhism. After the Buddha appeared, Buddhism came into being, but there was not as yet any division into sects or schools. Sectarianism is a limited view, a view of small scope, and cannot represent Buddhism in its entirety. The complete substance of Buddhism, the totality, admits no such divisions. When you divide the totality of Buddhism into sects and schools, you merely split it into fragments. In order to understand Buddhism in its totality, one must eliminate views of sects and schools and return to original Buddhism. One must return to the root and go back to the source.

KR: That brings me to a question about the different teachings taught here at Gold Mountain Monastery. I understand that you teach five different schools, including the Ch'an School, the Teaching School, the Vinaya School, the Secret School, and the Pure Land School. Can they all be taught like this together? Do they all belong to the original corpus of Buddhist teachings?

M: The Five Schools were created by Buddhist disciples who had nothing to do and wanted to find something with which to occupy their time. The Five Schools all issued from Buddhism. Since they came forth from Buddhism, they can return to Buddhism as well. Although the Five Schools serve different purposes, their ultimate destination is the same. It is said:

> *There is only one road back to the source,*
> *But there are many expedient ways to reach it.*

Although there are five different schools, they are still included within one "Buddhism". If you want to understand the totality of Buddhism, you need not divide it up into schools or sects. Originally there were no such divisions. Why make trouble when there is none? Why be divisive and cause people to have even more false thoughts than they already have?

People think that the Five Schools are something really special and wonderful. In fact, they have never departed from Buddhism itself. It's just like the government of a country. The government is made up of different departments. There is a Department of Health, a Department of Economics, a State Department, a Department of the Interior, and so forth. People may not realize that all these different departments are under a single government. All they recognize is the department, and they don't recognize the government as a whole. Their outlook is narrow. Now, we wish to move from the branches back to the roots. In the analogy, the roots are the government and the branches are the various departments. People should not abandon the roots and cling to the branches. If you only see the individual departments and fail to recognize the government, you will never be able to understand the problems faced by the country as a whole. You'll have no idea what they are all about.

KR: Then one should feel free to pursue any or all of the teachings?

M : Of course. Religion can't be allowed to tie one up.

KR: And if one chooses to follow only one certain school, can one reach the goal that all of them aim for?

M : All roads lead to Rome. All roads come to San Francisco. All roads will take you to New York. You may ask, 'Can I get to New York by this road?' but you would do better to ask yourself, 'Will I walk that road or not?'.

The following chapters cover three of the most widely practiced schools of Buddhism.

The Great Master Hui Neng,
Sixth Chan Patriarch in China[1]

Chapter Six

The Chan (Zen) School

Once when Shakyamuni Buddha was about to speak the Dharma, the Great Brahma Heaven King[2] presented him with a golden lotus. The Buddha held up the flower before the assembly without saying anything. At that time, the hundreds of thousands of gods and people who were present were silent, unaware of its significance. Only Mahakashyapa[3] responded by smiling. Then the Buddha said,

> *"I have the Treasury of the Proper Dharma Eye, the wondrous mind of Nirvana, the Reality beyond appearances, a subtle and wondrous Dharma-door, which is not based on the written or spoken word. It is a special transmission outside the teachings. I entrust this to Mahakashyapa."*[4]

This event 2500 years ago was the beginning of the Chan (Zen) School. The Japanese word "Zen" comes from the word "Chan" in Chinese. The word Chan itself is a transliterated and abbreviated version of the Sanskrit word "Dhyana". Originally the Chinese took the word Dhyana and transliterated it as Chan Na. Later they shortened it to just Chan.

Chan is distinguished by four characteristics:

1. It is not established by words,
2. It is a special transmission outside the teachings,
3. It directly points to the human mind,
4. Through it one sees one's own nature and becomes a Buddha.

Chan is transmitted directly from one mind to another mind. Its teaching simply directs the individual to see one's own inherent, true mind, referred to as "seeing the nature and returning to the source." That is, the enlightened teacher, profoundly aware of the mind of his student, certifies that the student's mind is indeed truly "awakened". This is a direct certification, mind to mind, that can only be done by a Sage.

Chan is also known as the "unfixed teaching," because both the means and the ends of Chan focus on non-attachment and subduing the ordinary "mad" mind that habitually tries to fix and shape reality to fit its own whims and preconceptions. A genuine and skilled Chan master employs a creative variety of techniques, tests, and teachings to help the student "stop the mad mind". These techniques can range from riddles, humor, and gentle scoldings to unorthodox strategies like total silence, expulsion from the monastery, or a slap in the face. The techniques themselves hold no significance or special power, rather their effectiveness lies in being uniquely suited to a particular individual at a particular time. The success of the unfixed teaching depends completely on the teacher's wisdom to spot what is appropriate to transform the student and the timing of delivery. These methods can take many different forms, but the results are identical: healthy, spiritual growth.

One bestows the teachings
for the sake of the individual.
One prescribes the medicine
according to the illness.

All of the ancient Chan Patriarchs from Mahakashyapa up through the Tang Dynasty, some 1200 years later when the Chan School branched out into five separate lineages, were outstanding members of the Bhikshu Sangha. Stern and pure in their upholding of the moral discipline, they taught by their unassailable life-style, actual accomplishment, and genuine humility. They were exemplars of lofty virtue and profound practice.

During the Ming Dynasty (1368-1644 AD), the Great Master Han Shan wrote the following essay, that shows even during his time people with genuine realization in Chan were few. They are undoubtedly more rare in the present time.

Good Teachers are Hard to Find

In the past, when the Chan movement flourished, clear-eyed good and wise teachers abounded. The monks who investigated were many; so too the instances of genuine realization.

Now, however, it isn't Chan which is lacking, but rather, that good teachers are hard to find. Now the home of Chan has become lonely and desolate. It's been that way for a long time already. Sure, there are those who impulsively resolve to investigate Chan. And they may even be fortunate enough to meet good and wise teachers who employ provisional techniques to help them make progress according to their propensities, and certify them according to their potential. Nonetheless, these students have shallow faculties, and easily jump to the conclusion that they already have some attainment. Moreover, they do not believe in the Sagely Teachings of the Thus Come One, do not seek the true and proper path, and insist on muddling along in their own confusion. Consequently they settle for cheap imitation "seals of approval". Not only do such people delude themselves, they misguide others as well. Isn't this something to be apprehensive about?

Moreover, prime ministers and others among the laity, who had some level of attainment as recorded in the <u>Annals of the Transmission of the Light</u> (1004-1107 AD) were just a handful. Within the wearisome dust of this present age, there are those who can't even uphold the major precepts[5], and whose false thinking is wild and turbid. And yet, relying on their worldly intelligence, they read a few of the records of the virtuous ones of old and start believing that they themselves have unsurpassed superior faculties. Thereupon they become extremely conceited and, thinking themselves already enlightened, engage monks in a Chan battle of wits. This is a sickness of the times; it's a case of one blind person leading a hoard of blind people.

Today this old monk has pointed out some essential aspects of working hard at cultivation as was practiced by the Buddha and the Patriarchs. Those of you who are clear-headed and intelligent should rectify yourselves according to these standards.

The purpose of including this essay in this introduction is to emphasize that genuine attainment in Chan requires hard work and long effort under a good teacher. Moreover, genuine attainment is difficult to recognize as it manifests in a self-effacing, low profile. Someone with true achievement does not wish to advertise or call attention to himself / herself. A teacher's only concern is to carry on the teachings by training students sincerely motivated to walk the Way.

Patience, No Greed, and Perseverance:
Three Requisites for Sitting in Meditation

...by Venerable Master Hsuan Hua[6]

Patience

What must you be patient with? You must learn to bear the pain in your back and the pain in your legs. When you first begin to sit in Chan meditation, you will experience pain in your back and legs because you are unaccustomed to sitting that way. In the beginning this pain may be hard to bear, so you have to be patient.

No Greed

Those who investigate Chan should not hope for enlightenment. If you think about how you want to become enlightened, then even if you were meant to get enlightened, that single thought will obstruct your enlightenment and prevent it from happening.

Furthermore, you should not, because of greed, seek for quick results in your practice. It's not that you can sit today and get enlightened tomorrow. So many of today's young people are turned upside-down, and although they want to investigate Chan and study the Buddhadharma, they take drugs which they say is a means of becoming enlightened fast. This is a grave mistake. Not only will such people not get enlightened, the more they study in this way, the more confused they become.

Therefore, I stress to you; don't try to get a bargain. Don't try to do it fast. Don't think that without putting out any effort you can cash in on welfare. There is nothing of value obtained without working for it.

Perseverance

You must be constant in your practice of Chan. The best way to sit is in full-lotus. Full-lotus simply requires placing your left ankle on your right thigh, and then lifting your right ankle onto your left thigh. This posture can quiet your mind. It is your foundation in sitting in Chan. You should train yourself to sit that way. Some of you protest,

"My legs are stiff and I can't sit that way."

Well, then try sitting in "half" lotus, which is when your left ankle is on your right thigh.

"But I can't even do that!" some may say.

Well, then you'll just have to sit in a cross-legged position, in whatever way is possible for you. But you should be working to get into half-lotus and eventually into full-lotus. Full-lotus is the foundation for sitting in meditation. Since it is fundamental, work to master it. If you try to build a house on bare ground, the first big rain that comes along will wash it away. The first big wind that blows will dismantle it. The same is true for meditation without a foundation.

Once your legs are in full-lotus, hold your body erect. Sit up straight, head looking straight ahead, and do not lean forward or backward; do not incline to the left or right. Keep your spine absolutely straight. Curl your tongue back against the roof of your mouth. Then if you salivate you can swallow the saliva. So, people who cultivate Chan should also not smoke cigarettes or take drugs because they turn your saliva bitter.

Your eyes are neither completely open nor closed. If you leave your eyes open while meditating, it is very easy to have false thinking about what you see. If you completely close your eyes while sitting, it is very easy to fall asleep. So keeping your eyes partially open is a good way to counteract both problems.

As to your mind — don't think of anything. Don't entertain any false thoughts. Don't think about what state you are experiencing or hope to experience, and don't think about how you want to get enlightened. The affairs of this world are not that simple. A thief who steals others' money ends up with wealth that is not his own. If you work and earn money then the wealth you accumulate is your own. The same principle applies to Chan. Don't be greedy for quick results, hoping to become enlightened fast. Don't be greedy to get a bargain. If in your cultivation you are greedy for small benefits, then you will never get the big ones.

Meditation, like all cultivation, must be practiced daily without interruption.

"But when will I be enlightened?" you ask.

It all depends on how hard you work. If you investigate all day from morning to night, while walking, standing, sitting, and lying down, your skill will mature and you will certainly become enlightened. For example, you can't see the trees grow, but every day they become taller. Meditation is like the wild grass growing in the spring: you can't see it grow, but daily it becomes more profuse.

Of course, everyone wants to become enlightened quickly, but if you don't do the work, how can you? When you went to school, you passed through grades from elementary school to high school to the University and then perhaps went on to get a Master's or a Doctorate. It's much harder to become a Buddha.

A Verse from the Song of Enlightenment
by the Great Master Yung Chia (7th Century),
with an explanation by the
Venerable Master Hsuan Hua

Dharma wealth is lost; merit and virtue destroyed,
Due to nothing else than the conscious mind.
Through the door of Chan the mind comes to rest,
And one suddenly enters the powerful, unborn
knowledge and vision.

Explanation: Why is it that cultivators of the spiritual path are not successful? Why don't they get a response from their sitting or other methods they happen to cultivate? Why is it that although we do meritorious deeds we lose our merit and virtue? It happens for no other reason than this: our conscious mind acts up. Our "mind" engages in false thinking; our "intellect" is busy calculating; and our "consciousness" is busy discriminating. Because our thoughts have not become focused and concentrated, we can not "quiet our thoughts".

Sitting in Chan is called "the quieting of thoughts". It means putting all errant thoughts to a complete rest. However, it's not easy for us to stop our automatic thinking system. The invisible wind of karma stirs up the sea of consciousness — huge billows and waves surge up, one wave after another without cease. Do our false thoughts have a physical appearance? No. You may be aware they are there, but upon further scrutiny, you discover that they have no substance. Our false thoughts fly everywhere, from one place to the next, like ocean waves crashing on the shore. Sometimes they resemble huge breakers; other times they are like small ripples. At ordinary times we are unaware of these false thought–waves because we live right in the midst of them and therefore do not

78

recognize them as false thoughts. However, when we sit quietly, even for a short moment, we become aware of how these uncountable numbers of thoughts surge up in our minds like countless waves on the ocean.

Therefore, The Song of Enlightenment says, *Dharma wealth is lost, merit and virtue destroyed, due to nothing other than the conscious mind.* When our thoughts are not focused, and we indulge in casual discrimination, then our eighth consciousness is torn by many thoughts of right and wrong, which rise and sink like waves. Because the mind, intellect, and consciousness are so busily involved in discursive thinking and speculation, we have an uncountable number of false thoughts. As a result, our Dharma wealth and merit and virtue are completely lost.

Through the door of Chan the mind comes to rest. The door of Chan refers to the Dharma-door, the method, of investigating Chan, in which one doesn't pursue the discriminations of the intellect, but instead brings all thoughts to a single focus, thereby quieting the mind. Then the mind reaches a state of unadulterated purity. For this reason, in the Chan School we investigate a meditation topic, such as "What was my original face before my parents gave birth to me?" Actually, the meditation topic is also a false thought. That being so, why do we still want to use it? Because the meditation topic is a "mantra" to keep the monkey (the mind) in check. If we didn't have a method to keep the monkey in check, then this monkey would scamper all about with wild abandon, jumping up and down. We might investigate "Who is mindful of the Buddha?" and try to find out "*who* is reciting Amitabha".

Someone might answer, "*It's me* who's reciting!".

Well, you say you are reciting, but have you ever seen this person who is reciting? Do you recognize who you truly are? Your present body is a false union of the four elements of earth, water, fire, and air. When those four elements disperse, where have *you* gone to?

For this reason, we look into " Who is mindful of the Buddha?" We bore into our topic, as if using a drill. The tougher the resistance, the more steadfastly we have to bore through. We investigate, boring deeper and deeper into this question until:

The mountains crumble and the waters dry up
And it's uncertain whether there's a road ahead at all
Then right in the shadow of the willows and bright flowers
appears another village.[7]

To put it in a nutshell: Chan is not manipulated or controlled by the discriminating consciousness.

And suddenly one enters the powerful, unborn knowledge and vision. Before you have understood, then even when you are sitting in Chan you are constantly engaged in false thinking, and that way, will never become enlightened. The requirement for enlightenment is concentration. If all the false thoughts in your head can cease, then your true wisdom will be revealed. Becoming enlightened means to understand; to no longer be deluded.

Those of you who sit in Chan, don't be afraid of the pain in your legs or back. Have a vajra-like resolve. Use the three qualities of firmness, sincerity, and perseverance. Be resolute, unchanging, and constant in your effort. The virtuous monks of ancient times would practice sitting for several decades. This work is not simple. It's not like you can "have peonies today and trade them for lotuses tomorrow". You cannot be enlightened in only one day of meditation. You must develop patience and always attend classes on Chan.

And in what way should you practice meditation? Look at the way a girl pursues her boyfriend or a boy pursues his girlfriend. If you can use the same kind of fervor and dedication in every passing thought during the investigation of your meditation topic, then you will obtain success without fail.

[1]Although the Master was illiterate, he had reached a profound level of Enlightenment. As one of the greatest Chan Masters, he is so venerated that the record of his life and teachings, known as the *Sixth Patriarch Sutra*, is considered to be a canonical text.

[2]The Brahma Heaven King is the ruler over the First Dhyana Heavens. See Appendix I under the Form Realm Heaven for further information.

[3]Mahakashyapa was one of the Buddha's great disciples. He was foremost in the cultivation of ascetic practices.

[4]*Sutra of the Great Brahma Heaven King Questioning the Buddha to Resolve his Doubts.*

[5]See Chapter 3 for detailed explanation of the Five Moral Precepts.

[6]This instructional talk appears in *Listen To Yourself, Think it Over*, Volume 2, BTTS.

[7]A common Buddhist saying in China. Origin unknown.

The Buddha Amitabha (Limitless Light)

in the Western World, Ultimate Happiness

Chapter Seven

Pure Land School

Moreover, Shariputra, in that Buddhaland there is always divine music and the ground is yellow gold. In the six periods of the day and night a heavenly rain of mandarava (white lotus)flowers fall, and throughout the clear morning, each living being of that land, offers sacks full of the myriad of wonderful flowers, to the hundreds of billions of Buddhas in the other directions....

Shariputra, in that Buddhaland when the soft wind blows, the rows of jeweled trees and jeweled nets give forth subtle and wonderful sounds, like one hundred thousand kinds of music played in symphony. The hearts of all those who hear are naturally inspired with mindfulness of the Buddha, mindfulness of the Dharma, and mindfulness of the Sangha....[1]

A Buddha's "Pure Land" is a world-system imbued with many special characteristics: the three evil destinies of the hells, ghosts and animals are absent; the earth is gentle and even; the landscape beautiful and distinctively lovely. Life there resembles our vision of living in blissful heaven. Yet, unlike the heavens, the luxury and grandeur of a Pure Land is designed to inspire in the inhabitants mindfulness of the Triple Jewel. Dwellers there always get to hear the Buddha and his retinue of Bodhisattvas teaching the Dharma. All beings born in the Pure Lands eventually become Buddhas themselves in other world-systems, or they purposely remain high Bodhisattvas to help living beings. Once born in a Pure Land one never again falls into the three lower realms of existence or retreats from the Buddha's path.

Amitabha Buddha established a Pure Land called the "Land of Ultimate Happiness", situated billions of worlds-systems from us in the west. Amitabha means "Measureless Light" and Amitayus, another one of his names, means "Measureless Life". Beings in our world have close affinities with Amitabha Buddha, therefore our Buddha, Shakyamuni, spoke the *Amitabha Sutra* on our behalf. The *Amitabha Sutra* will be the last Sutra to remain in our world as the Dharma declines. After the *Amitabha Sutra* disappears, the only Buddhadharma remaining in the world will be the words "Namo (Homage to) Amitabha Buddha". These words will survive for one hundred years bringing liberation to limitless beings who sincerely recite them. After that, only the words "Amitabha Buddha" will endure as an efficacious method for seeking liberation. After another hundred years Amitabha Buddha's name will disappear leaving no more Buddha-dharma in our world, until the next Buddha, Maitreya, appears in about ten million years.

This explains why the method of reciting the name of Amitabha Buddha is considered to be so important in Buddhism. There are three prerequisites for being reborn in the Land of Ultimate Happiness.

1. Faith. There must be a basic faith in oneself: that by turning away from the bad and going towards the good we can transform ourselves to a degree that merits this superior rebirth. We also, must believe the Pure Land does indeed exist.

In Buddhism faith is extremely important. It says in the *Flower Adornment Sutra*,

Faith is the source of the Path,
the mother of merit and virtue.
It nurtures all good dharmas.[2]

2. Vows. We must make vows to be reborn in the Pure Land, and also, make great vows to benefit all sentient beings.

3. Practice. We need to really cultivate the Buddha's teachings, and diligently recite the Buddha's name.

The Buddha said that one who wishes to be reborn in Amitabha Buddha's Pure Land must cultivate the following virtues:

First, one must be filial to and serve one's parents, respect teachers and elders, have a kind heart and not kill any being, and practice the ten kinds of good karma.[3]

Second, one must receive the three refuges (taking refuge in the Triple Jewel), and perfect the various moral regulations.

Third, one must resolve to become Enlightened, have deep faith in cause and effect, recite the Great Vehicle Sutras, and diligently practice according to them.[4]

In the *Sixth Patriarch Sutra*, the Great Chan Master Hui Neng said,

Common, deluded people do not understand their inherent nature and do not know that the Pure Land is within themselves. Therefore they make vows for the East and West. To enlightened people, all places are the same. As the Buddha said, "In whatever place one dwells, there is constant peace and happiness."

If the mind-ground is only without unwholesomeness,

85

the West is not far from here. If one harbors unwholesome thoughts, one may recite the Buddha's name, but it will be difficult to be reborn there.

Instructions on Reciting the Buddha's Name
by the Venerable Master Hsuan Hua

The reason this simple method is so efficacious is that in former lives, when Amitabha Buddha was cultivating, he practiced many Dharmas and suffered innumerable bitter experiences — all of which he found difficult to use and perfect. Accordingly, he made forty eight great vows, one of which states that any person who recites his name will be assured rebirth in his world system in the West, the Pure Land of Ultimate Happiness, and there become enlightened. Our recitation is like sending a telegram to Amitabha Buddha in the West. At the end of our lives, the Bodhisattvas will guide us to be reborn in his Western Pure Land.

From morning to night, moving or quiet, at all times, you can recite. While moving, you can recite and change motion into stillness; when still, you can recite and turn stillness into motion. When there is neither motion nor stillness, your telegram to Amitabha Buddha has gotten through and you've received his response.

If you maintain your recitation with undivided attention morning and night without stopping, you may recite to the point that you don't know that you are walking when you walk, you don't feel thirst when you are thirsty, and you don't experience hunger when you are hungry, you don't know you are cold in freezing weather, and you don't notice the heat in hot weather. People and things are empty, and you and Amitabha Buddha become one. 'Amitabha Buddha is me and I am Amitabha Buddha.' The two cannot be separated. Recite single-mindedly and sincerely without false thinking. Pay no attention to worldly concerns. When you don't know the time and don't know the day, you may arrive at a miraculous state.

You may ask, "But isn't that just being dumb?"

In fact, rather than having become dumb, you will have experienced 'great wisdom which seems like stupidity'.

The Bodhisattva Great Strength explains the practice of reciting the Buddha's name in the *Shurangama Sutra*, (Volume 5):

If two people remember each other until the memory of each is deep, then in life after life they will be together like a form and its shadow, and they will never be at odds.

Out of pity for living beings, the Thus Come Ones of the ten directions are mindful of them as a mother remembers her child. If the child runs away, what use is the mother's regard for him ? But if the child remembers his mother in the same way that she remembers him, then in life after life the mother and child will not be far apart.

If living beings are always mindful of the Buddha, certainly they will see the Buddha now or in the future. They will never be far from the Buddha, and their minds will awaken by themselves, without the aid of expedient methods.

[1]*Amitabha Sutra*, BTTS.

[2]*Worthy Leader,* Chapter 12, *Flower Adornment Sutra.*

[3]The ten kinds of good karma are: not killing, not stealing, not engaging in sexual misconduct, abstaining from lying, gossiping, abusive speech, and back-biting speech, and not having thoughts of greed, hatred, and stupidity.

[4]*The Sutra of Contemplating Measureless Life Buddha.*

The Bodhisattva Observer of the Worlds' Sounds (Avalokiteshvara), Foremost in Compassion

Chapter Eight

The Secret School

The Secret School derives its name from the fact that the response that one receives from the power of reciting mantras is secret. No one can tell you about it. You must cultivate it yourself and then you will know the mantra's influence for yourself; just as when you drink water you yourself know whether it is warm or cold. It is not that the mantras themselves are secret.

The Secret School specializes in holding mantras. Mantras have the following four meanings:[1]

1. All mantras are the names of god and ghost kings. When you recite the names of the god and ghost kings, the small gods and ghosts are well-behaved, and do not dare to cause you trouble. Why? It is because they wonder, "How do you know our ghost king? How do you know our god king?"

2. Mantras are also like a soldier's password. In the army there is a different password every day. Only your own people know it and the people outside do not. Let's say the password is "victory". If you meet a soldier whom you do not know, then you ask him what the password is. If he says "victory", then you say "right". You know that he is one of us. But if you ask him the password and he says "lucky", you know that he is not one of us. Mantras work the same way. As soon as the gods and ghosts hear you recite the mantra, they say, "Oh, that is our password," so they are all well-behaved. Otherwise they would want to fight with you.

3. Mantras are a kind of secret language, which only certain people understand. An analogy will make this clear. Suppose there is a person who is very poor and lowly. He goes abroad where people do not know him. He tells them, "I am the king of a certain country, but the generals revolted and there was a change of government. I secretly escaped and came to this country." The king of this country really does not know whether he is genuine or not. He's a phony, but the king thinks that he is genuine, so he gives him one of the princesses for a wife. This makes him a prince, a member of the king's household. He wasn't a king before, but he acts like it. Day in and day out he is always losing his temper.

Then a person comes to this country who knows that this impostor was a poor and lowly person, and says to the princess who is married to him, "When he gets angry, you need only say these few sentences: 'Originally you were a poor and lowly person who drifted in from another country far away. Why must you have such a big temper?' As soon as you say this, he will know, 'Oh, she knows my humble origins,' and will not get angry anymore." A mantra has the same effect. As soon as you recite the mantra, the gods and ghosts will assume that you understand their origins, that you know what they are all about, and so they will not dare to cause you trouble.

4. Mantras are the mind-imprint of all Buddhas. "Mind-imprint" alludes to the way in which the minds of two enlightened beings interact and acknowledge each other. They are the secret language of all Buddhas which can only be known by them. Because all other living beings do not understand them, mantras are left untranslated.

In the Sutras it clearly explains that people who keep mantras must very carefully uphold the moral regulations. For example, the Buddha, in the *Shurangama Sutra*, gave these instructions on what is required for mantra cultivation:

> *To do so, they must find as their teacher a foremost Shramana (Bhikshu) who is pure in the precepts. If they do not encounter a member of the Sangha who is truly pure, then it is absolutely certain that their deportment in moral precepts cannot be perfected. After perfecting the precepts, they should put on fresh, clean clothes, light incense in a place where they are alone, and recite the spiritual mantra spoken by the Buddha of the mind[2] one hundred and eight times.*

And in the *Sutra of the Bodhisattva's Wholesome Precepts* it says:

> *One who receives and keeps this spiritual mantra (Shurangama Mantra) is prohibited from eating meat, or the five pungent plants (garlic, onions, leeks, chives and scallions); taking intoxicants; engaging in sexual misconduct; eating or drinking in impure abodes.[3]*

And in the *Sutra of the Inquiries of Wonderful Arms Bodhisattva* it says:

> *If in reciting and keeping the mantra (Shurangama Mantra) one violates propriety, or if one does not keep the moral precepts, or if one is not pure, not only will one be unsuccessful with this Dharma, one will bring harm upon oneself.[4]*

A person who follows the moral regulations and diligently practices mantra recitation achieves a great deal within the Dharma. In the *Great Compassion Heart Dharani Sutra,* Bodhisattva Observer of the World's Sounds[5] says:

If you can apply your mind with pure sincerity, maintain vegetarianism and the moral precepts, and repent of and reform all your past offenses on behalf of living beings; if you can repent and confess your own various evil acts committed throughout countless eons past; and if you can recite the Dharani continuously, without skipping a single sound, then in this very life you may certify to the four fruits of a Shramana[6]. You will be endowed with a keen disposition, wise contemplation, and expedient methods. You will obtain the status of the Ten Grounds[7] without difficulty. Even more will you be rewarded with small blessings. You will obtain everything you seek.

OM MANI PADME HUM
By Tripitaka Master Hsuan Hua[8]

These six words together make up the Brilliant Mantra of Six Words. Each word is able to emit brilliant light. Mantra study and practice comes under the province of the Secret School, one of the five major divisions or "schools" of the Buddha's teachings. The five schools are:

1. The Chan School
2. The Teaching (Scholastic) School
3. The Vinaya (Ethics) School
4. The Secret School
5. The Pure Land School.

The Chan School exclusively investigates Chan (Dhyana or Zen) meditation. The Teaching School emphasizes scholastic inquiry, exegesis, lecturing sutras and interpreting and expounding Dharma. The Vinaya School focuses on questions of ethics and cultivating moral self-discipline. Vinaya students strive to be "awesome, majestic, and pure in Vinaya, great models for the three realms of existence". Then there is the Secret School. "Secret" means "no mutual knowing". And finally, the Pure Land School teaches the exclusive mindfulness and recitation of "Na Mo A Mi To Fwo" ('Homage to Amitabha Buddha') the "Vast Six Character Name".

Some people say the Chan School is the highest of the five. Others claim that the Teaching School, or the Vinaya School, is highest. Cultivators of the Secret School say "The Secret School is supreme". Practitioners of the Pure Land Dharma-door say, "The Pure Land Dharma door is first, it is superior". Actually, all Dharmas are equal; there is no high or low. "Highest" is everyone's own personal opinion; whatever school you like, you claim to be the highest.

Now I will explain the Secret School. In fact, the Secret School is not secret. Within the secret teaching, the apparent and the secret perfectly penetrate. The apparent teaching also includes the Secret School. For example, the Great Compassion Mantra and the Bril liant Mantra of Six Words both belong to the Secret School. The Shurangama Mantra is even more "secret".

Foolish people say that secret things are the best. Why? Because they are secret, and they are not available to everyone. So people who don't understand Buddhism speak of the supernatural and mysterious saying, "Oh! I can't tell this to you! It's from the Secret School, and it can't be spoken for you to hear!" If they can't speak of it to others, why mention it? Why do they say they can't talk about it? If it's really the Secret School, and it's best not to speak of it, why do they say, "I can't tell you"? Their "not talking" is just talking about it. Isn't this refusal to speak of it, speaking of it? Why do they talk this way? Because they don't understand the Buddha-dharma, and are completely unaware of what the Secret

School really signifies.

Now I will tell you something about the Secret School. It's not that mantras are secret. The Secret School is the efficacious response which comes from *your* recitation of mantras; I can't know your response. I recite mantras and have my efficacious response, and you do not know of it. This is "no mutual knowing". The ability and power are unfathomable and unknown, and are therefore called the Secret School. It's not the mantras themselves, but the power of mantras that is secret. This is the meaning of the Secret School.

If mantras are really secret, they should not be transmitted to other people; for if you transmit a mantra to someone else, it is no longer secret. It is the same as the Sixth Patriarch's answer to Hui Ming's question:

"He (Hui Ming) further asked, 'Apart from the above secret speech and secret meaning, is there yet another secret meaning?' Hui Neng said, 'What has been spoken to you is not secret. If you return the light and look within (examine yourself) the secret is yours.'"

Speak it and it is not secret. Take a look; he said it very clearly. Once spoken, it is no longer secret. The "secret" is that which is not transmitted. If it can be transmitted, it is not "secret". The secret can not be transmitted; it is on your side, within you; it is where you are.

I believe that even many Secret School Dharma Masters do not understand how to explain "secret" dharma correctly. They think that mantras are secret. But all mantras can be orally transmitted to people; there are no mantras which cannot be spoken. If they couldn't be spoken, there would be no way to transmit them. Isn't that right? If it is transmittable, it is not secret — and by that odd logic, it would no longer be the Secret School. Because the "secret" is untransmittable, I say that the "secret" is the mantra's power, and there is no way anyone can tell you about it. No one can say, "This mantra has this power, and when you recite it, such and such will happen." There is no way to explain it. It is like drinking water; you yourself know whether it is hot or cold. The "secret" is what you know and others do not. The power is secret, the response is secret, the subjective experience is secret; it is not the mantra that is secret. Now does everyone understand?

Many people who don't understand Buddhism think I have spoken incorrectly about this dharma. Incorrect or not, I will still speak this way. And if you say I am right...there is no way for you to say that, either. Since you basically do not understand this dharma, how can you say that I understand? I don't understand, I'm even more confused. Previously, however, I had a teacher who taught me with great clarity so that I understood, and this confused person changed into one who could speak and explain the Brilliant Mantra of Six Words according to the Secret School.

The Secret School is divided into five divisions, East, West, North, South and Center. In the East is the Vajra Division, which protects and maintains the proper Dharma; in the South is the Jeweled Production Division; the West, the Lotus Division; the North, the Karma Division; and in the Center, the Buddha Division. The Shurangama Mantra explains these five divisions in great detail.

If there is one person who can recite the Shurangama Mantra, the demon kings cannot appear in the world. If no one can recite it, demons can enter all of the billion world systems. Why? Because no one watches over them; no one works in the five divisions, so the demons are able to infiltrate the world. If one person, however,

97

can recite the Shurangama Mantra, demons dare not enter. It is just because of this that we hope more people will learn to recite the Shurangama Mantra. During the first summer session, the first test was to recite the Shurangama Mantra from memory; two people were able to do so. Later, many more were able to recite the mantra from memory. Now I will talk about the Brilliant Mantra of Six Words.

The first word is "Om". When you recite "Om" once, all ghosts and spirits must place their palms together because this signifies their intent to maintain the rules and regulations. By conforming to the regulations, they stay on the proper way. Recite this once and all ghosts and spirits do not dare rebel and create confusion; they do not dare disobey orders. This is the first sound in the mantra.

"Mani" means "silent wisdom". Using wisdom one is able to understand all truths, and thus abide in the state of quiescence that is without birth. It is also defined as, "separating from filth", which means living a morally pure life free of defilement. It can be compared to the "precious as-you-will pearl" which is extremely pure and immaculate. Whatever you wish to excel in can be done if you have the "precious as you-will pearl". It can also fulfill your wishes in accord with your thoughts. Every vow you make will be fulfilled. These are its benefits.

"Padme" means "light perfectly illuminating", and is also defined as "the opening of the lotus". This is the wonderful mind of Avalokiteshvara Bodhisattva. This is "Padme".

Next comes "Hum", which means to "give rise to". Anything at all can be created from this character "Hum". It also means "to protect and support". Recite this word and all Dharma protectors and good spirits come to support and protect you. It also means "eradicating disasters". Recite this word and whatever difficulties you encounter will be eradicated. It also means "success"; whatever you cultivate can be accomplished.

Recite the Brilliant Mantra of Six Words once, and the immeasurable Buddhas, Bodhisattvas, and Vajra Dharma protectors support and protect you. Therefore, when Avalokiteshvara Bodhisattva finished saying this Brilliant Mantra of Six Words, there were seven million Buddhas who came to support, protect, and surround him. The power and capacity of the Brilliant Mantra of Six Words are inconceivable; "the Path and the response intertwine in an inconceivable way." Therefore it is called the Secret School. If one were to explain in detail, the meanings would be limitless and boundless. They cannot be completely spoken. So I have just given this simple explanation for everyone.

Now I will tell you a little about what cannot be told of the Secret School's power. Why do I say "what cannot be told"? Because my talking does not even comprise one ten-thousandth part of it. What is it? If you are able to constantly recite and maintain the Brilliant Mantra of Six Words, the darkness of the six paths of existence will change into bright light. You must be single-minded when reciting this mantra to achieve this type of samadhi. Then, not only will the six paths of existence emit light, but all of the ten dharma realms will become the "a great storehouse of light". So now we know something of the power of the Brilliant Mantra of Six Words. I hope everyone will set aside time from their activities to recite the Brilliant Mantra of Six Words.

[1]Excerpted from lectures by the Venerable Tripitaka Master Hsuan Hua.
[2]*Shurangama Sutra*, Volume 6, BTTS.

[3]*Shurangama Mantra,* Volume. 1, BTTS.

[4]ibid.

[5]Observer of the Worlds Sounds is a translation of Chinese Kuan Shih Yin and Sanskrit Avalokiteshvara.

[6]The four fruits of a Shramana are the four levels of Arhats. See explanation in Chapter 5, under "Sangha of the Sages".

[7]The Ten Grounds are the levels of Enlightenment immediately preceding Equal Enlightenment and the complete Enlightenment of a Buddha. See Chapter 5, under "Sangha of the Sages," for a brief description of the Bodhisattva's Enlightenment. Refer to *Flower Adornment Sutra, Ten Grounds,* Chapter 26, Volume One and Two, BTTS, for a detailed explanation of the Ten Grounds.

[8]This lecture appeared in the periodical of Buddhist studies, *Vajra Bodhi Sea,* Issue No. 11, February, 1971.

Introduction to Chart of *Samsara*

The chart on the following pages lists the states of existence within *Samsara,* the realm of birth and death. In *Samsara* there are three distinct levels of existence. The highest is the Formless Realm, in which there are the greatest gods who have transcended the physical body, having mentality only. There are four heavens on this level.

The next level, the Form Realm, also, only consists of heavens. The gods in these eighteen heavens have a form, but they have gone beyond the greed and lust for the pleasures of the five senses. They've attained a state of very profound and sublime happiness that it is a result of their skill in meditative concentration. Their greed for the five senses has been eclipsed by means of the force of their concentration-power. This is just like when a boulder is placed on grass, the grass is temporarily unable to grow. In the same way their meditative power and ability has temporarily suppressed their thirst for the pleasures of the five senses, but it is still latent. The only way it can be eliminated forever, is by means of prajna wisdom. The Sages, that is the Arhats and Bodhisattvas as mentioned in Chapter Five, attain permanent states of Enlightenment in which this greed is truly extinguished.

On the next level, the Realm of Sensual Desire, there are six heavens, the realms of Asuras, human beings, animals, ghosts, and the denizens of hell. The minds of all the beings in these states are dominated by the drive for sensual pleasures. Those in the heavens here enjoy an incredible happiness associated with the senses as a result of their practice of good karma in the past.

Those in the three lowest states, also known as the Three Evil Destinies, that is animals, ghosts, and denizens of the hell, undergo much suffering and difficulty.

As mentioned in the Introduction the purpose of the Buddha's teachings is to see that all states of existence in *Samsara* lack substantial reality. As it says in the *Shurangama Sutra* (Volume 7) they:

> *Come into being from false thoughts, and their subsequent karma comes from false thoughts. Within the wonderful perfection of the fundamental mind that is unconditioned, they are like strange flowers in space, for there is basically nothing to cling to. They are entirely vain and false, and they have no source or beginning.*

Chart Of *Samsara*
The Realm Of Birth And Death
Divided into the Three Realms of Existence

Key:
Kalpa=16 million years
Small Kalpa=1,000 Kalpas
Middle Kalpa=20 Small Kalpas
Great Kalpa=4 Middle Kalpas
Yojana= 28 Miles

Asankhyeya Mahakalpa=1.28 billion vigintillion or 1.28×10^{72} years

Our Buddha, Shakyamuni, in order to perfect his "blessings and wisdom", cultivated for many, many lifetimes in a period of time covering three Asankhyeya Mahakalpas. He then further practiced for 100 Great Kalpas to perfect the 32 Hallmarks and 80 Subsidiary Features of a Buddha.

Formless Realm

Name of Sphere of Existence	Average Lifespan	Average Height	Comments
Heaven of Neither Thought Nor Non-Thought	80,000 Great Kalpas (102.4 quadrillion years)		Gods in the Formless Heavens have no bodies. They only have consciousness.
Heaven of Nothing Whatsoever	60,000 Great Kalpas		
Heaven of Boundless Consciousness	40,000 Great Kalpas		
Heaven of Boundless Space	20.000 Great Kalpas		

Form Realm

Name of Sphere of Existence	Average Lifespan	Average Height	Comments
5 Heavens of No-Return:			
Ultimate Form Heaven	16,000 Great Kalpas (20.48 quadrillion years)	16,000 Yojanas (448,000 miles)	The Five Heavens of No-Return are also known as the Pure Abodes or Pure Dwellings. Gods in the Heavens of No-Return are Sages who have certified to the Third Stage of an Arhat. The gods of all the other heavens cannot even see these heavens, because they are beyond their scope.
Good Manifestation Heaven	8,000 Great Kalpas	8,000 Yojanas	
Good View Heaven	4,000 Great Kalpas	4,000 Yojanas	
No Heat Heaven	2,000 Great Kalpas	2,000 Yojanas	
No Affliction Heaven	1,000 Great Kalpas	1,000 Yojanas	
Fourth Dhyana Heavens:			
No Thought Heaven	500 Great Kalpas (640 trillion years)	500 Yojanas (14,000 miles)	These heavens correspond to the state of dhyana meditation called *Ground of Purity from Renouncing Thought.* In this state subtle thoughts cease.
Vast Fruit Heaven	500 Great Kalpas	500 Yojanas	
Love of Blessings Heaven	250 Great Kalpas	250 Yojanas	
Birth of Blessings Heaven	125 Great Kalpas	125 Yojanas	

Form Realm

Name of Sphere of Existence	Average Lifespan	Average Height	Comments
Third Dhyana Heavens:			
Pervasive Purity Heaven	64 Great Kalpas (81.92 trillion years)	64 Yojanas (1,792 miles)	These heavens correspond to the state of dhyana meditation called the *Ground of Wondrous Bliss from Leaving Joy.* In this state coarse thoughts cease.
Limitless Purity Heaven	32 Great Kalpas	32 Yojanas	
Lesser Purity Heaven	16 Great Kalpas	16 Yojanas	
Second Dhyana Heavens:			
Light-Sound Heaven	8 Great Kalpas (10.24 trillion years)	8 Yojanas (224 miles)	These heavens correspond to the state of dhyana meditation called the *Ground of Joy from Producing Samadhi.* In this state outer breath ceases. Beings in the Light-Sound Heaven use light to speak, the way a TV uses light to create pictures.
Limitless Light Heaven	4 Great Kalpas	4 Yojanas	
Lesser Light Heaven	2 Great Kalpas	2 Yojanas	
First Dhyana Heavens:			
Great Brahma Heaven	3 Middle Kalpas (960 billion years)	1 1/2 Yojanas (42 miles)	These heavens correspond to the *Ground of Joy Arising from Separation.* In this state the pulse stops.
Ministers of Brahma Heaven	2 Middle Kalpas	1 Yojana	
Multitudes of Brahma Heaven	1 Middle Kalpa	1/2 Yojana	

All the gods in the Form Realm Heavens are without the sense of smell and taste, and they do not eat food, sleep, or have sexual desire. However, the desires for these things are still latent and once their heavenly life comes to an end, they can still return to any lower realm of existence in accordance with their karma. These desires are also latent in the gods in the Formless Heavens. The Third and Fourth Stage Arhats and the Bodhisattvas, because of prajna wisdom, have ended these desires at their origin, so they will never arise again.

In the "comments" above, in the right-hand column, it describes specific things that happen to a human being who enters the levels of dhyana meditation which correspond to the Dhyana Heavens. In addition to the above, when one enters the First Dhyana meditation state one can sit for seven days without getting up from one's seat. At that time one can also go without eating, drinking or sleeping. In the Second Dhyana one can sit for 49 days. In the Third Dhyana one can sit for three years. And in the Fourth Dhyana one can sit for nine years. The happiness experienced in dhyana meditation far surpasses the happiness connected with the five senses.

Sensual Desire Realm

Name of Sphere of Existence	Average Lifespan	Average Height	Comments
Six Desire Heavens:			
Self-Mastery Over Others' Transformations Heaven	16,000 Heaven years (9.2 billion years)	4,500 feet 1 day=1,600 human years	They usurp others' happiness. Many demons and their retinues dwell here, like Mara, the king of demons.
Bliss From Transformations Heaven	8,000 Heaven years (2.3 billion years)	3,500 feet 1 day=800 human years	Can transform their own happiness. Food and clothing appear as they think about them.
Contentment (Tushita) Heaven	4,000 Heaven years (576 million years)	3,000 feet 1 day=400 human years	Heaven of "Joyful Contentment". Gods totally free from all worries—very content.
Well-Divided Time (Suyama) Heaven	2,000 Heaven years (144 million years)	2,250 feet 1 day=200 human years	Gods are always joyful, singing songs from morning till night: "Merrily indeed, I'm so happy!"
Heaven of the Thirty-three (Trayastrimsha)	1,000 Heaven years (36 million years)	1,500 feet 1 day= 100 human years	Ruled by Lord Shakra, King of Gods, also known as Indra, and the God of the Christian Bible.
Heaven of the Four Kings	500 Heaven years (9 million years)	750 feet 1 day=50 human years	Ruled by Four God kings—one in each direction. Newborns are as big as a 5 year old human.

Gods in the Desire Heavens still have desires connected with the five senses, including the desires for food, sleep and sex, with marriages as in the human realm. Yet the happiness they experience is much greater than that of the human realm. The human realm compared to even the lowest Desire Heaven is like a toilet pit. The gods in the first two Desire Heavens fulfill their sexual desire in the same way as those in the human realm. In the Suyama Heaven they fulfill it by holding hands. In the Tushita Heaven they fulfill it by smiling at each other, In the Bliss From Transformations Heaven it is fulfilled by mutual gazing. And the Heaven of Self-Mastery Over Others' Transformations it is fulfilled by merely glancing. All the heavens beginning with the Suyama Heaven and above do not have a sun or a moon. In those heavens, the bodies of these gods emit their own light.

Asuras

Although asuras are an individual realm by themselves, they also can appear in both of the other good paths of gods and humans as well as in the three evil destinies of the hells, the ghosts and animals. In general, regardless of what path they are in, they like to pick fights and have bad tempers. They enjoy bossing others around and like to be supervisors, but they can't stand being supervised by others. Among people, asuras can be good or bad. The good asuras include military officials and troops, and bad asuras are thieves, thugs, murderers and the like.

Asuras are unruly beings that love to fight. Their name means "ugly". It also means "ungodly" because, although some asuras enjoy heavenly blessings, nonetheless, they lack authority in the heavens.

There are four categories of asuras in the three realms of existence. Asuras in the path of ghosts use their strength to protect the Dharma and can with spiritual penetrations travel through space. They are born from eggs and belong to the destiny of ghosts.

Those who have fallen from virtue and been expelled from the heavens dwell in places near the sun and moon. They are asuras born from wombs and belong to the destiny of humans.

There are also asura kings who support the world with a penetrating power and fearlessness. They vie for position with the Brahma Lord, the God Shakra, and the Four Heavenly Kings. These asuras come into being by transformation and belong to the destiny of gods.

Ananda, there is another, base category of asuras. Their minds dwell in underwater caves. During the day they roam the skies; at night they return to their watery realm. These asuras come into being because of moisture and belong to the destiny of animals[1].

107

Human Beings

All Buddhas become Buddhas in the human realm. The human realm presents the best state of existence for spiritual cultivation because it has a balance of good and bad. In the three evil destinies (hells, animals, ghosts), intense suffering precludes any other awareness. One merely longs to escape the immediate agony, and is unable to consider the deeper significance of suffering as a universal condition of all the states of conditioned existence.

The Buddha once held up a clump of dirt in his hand and asked his disciples which was greater, the dirt in his hand, or the dirt of the whole earth. The disciples answered that of course the dirt of the earth was far greater than the dirt in the Buddha's hand. The Buddha said that those beings who secure a human form are like the dirt in his hand; whereas those who had human form but have lost it (regressing into the three evil destinies) are as many as the dirt covering the entire earth. Thus we see that human life is extremely precious and fragile.

The Three Evil Destinies

If you wish, you can enter the realms of existence mentioned above to try them out—put on a play—but you shouldn't play around with the three remaining realms. If you try these out you may not be able to escape. It is said that after one life in a human body, 10,000 kalpas may pass before that form can be obtained again. Playing around with the three evil destinies can be very dangerous.

Animals

Eager animals feed on greed,
Never sated by a lot.
Because they make what's black white,
They don't distinguish wrong from right.

There are billions of animals, an infinite variety—flying, crawling, swimming, and walking—on land, in the water and in the sky. Beings become animals as a result of one thing: greed. For them, no matter what it is, the more the better. Animals lack the ability to reason. They become muddled and ignorance envelops them so that they become totally oblivious to anything rational—even to the point that they are greedy to eat excrement.

Ghosts

The ghostly crew delights in hate,
Deluded by effects, confused about cause.
Their ignorance and upside-downness
Grows greater each day, deeper each month.

Almost everyone has heard of ghosts, but not everyone believes in them. Ghosts are masses of *yin* energy which have shadow and no form, or form and no shadow. There are as many different kinds of ghosts as there are grains of sand in the Ganges River. Some ghosts are affluent and reign as kings over the ghost realm; some ghosts are poverty stricken and devoid of authority—it is often the poor ghosts who bother people. If you want to investigate ghosts in detail, work hard at your spiritual cultivation, open the Five Eyes and Six Spiritual Penetrations[2], and then explore for yourself.

Hells

The hells' anxiety and suffering
Is devoid of doors yet one bores right in.
Giving rise to delusion deeds are done.
The retribution is born in due accord[3].

Anyone who would like to take a vacation in the hells can do so at any time at all. I can guarantee that. But the hells are a miserable place. Lamentation plants the seeds for hells; happiness plants the seeds for heavens. Unlike jails, the hells, although man-made by people who commit offenses, haven't any doors. However, if you are due to go to the hells, when you arrive it is just as if a door opened, because you find yourself worming and boring in where there was no entrance.

[1]*Shurangama Sutra*, Volume 7, BTTS.
[2]See Chapter 5 under "Sangha of the Sages" for an explanation of the Five Eyes and the Six Spiritual Penetrations.
[3]*The Ten Dharma Realms Are Not Beyond A Single Thought*, BTTS. The verses and the explanations of the Three Evil Destinies are excerpted from the Venerable Tripitaka Master Hsuan Hua's commentary on the *Ten Dharma Realms*.

The Bodhisattva Universal Worthy (Samantabhadra),

Foremost in Practice

Appendix II

The Ten Great Practices Of All Bodhisattvas

In the *Flower Adornment Sutra,* considered the king of kings of Sutras, the Buddha tells how all Bodhisattvas everywhere and throughout all time practice these ten conducts of the Bodhisattva Universal Worthy (Samantabhadra), in order to become Buddhas:

Worship all Buddhas

Before the Lions Among Men (the Buddhas)
throughout the worlds of the ten directions,
In the past, present, and future
With body, mouth, and mind entirely pure,
I bow before them all omitting none.

Praise the Thus Come Ones

With each oceanic sound I let fall everywhere
Words and phrases, wonderful and endless,
Which now through all the eons of the future,
Praise the wide, deep ocean of the
Buddha's merit and virtue.

Extensively Make Offerings

I vow to always meet the Thus Come Ones face to face
And the hosts of disciples who surround them.
Untiringly to the end of future time,
I'll make offerings to them vast and great.

Repent of and Reform Karmic Obstacles

All the evil deeds I've done
From beginningless ignorance, greed, and hate,
Created by my body, mouth and mind:
I now repent of and will reform them all.

Rejoice in and Follow Merit and Virtue

I rejoice in the merit and virtue
Of all beings in the ten directions,
Those still learning and those beyond,
And all Thus Come Ones and Bodhisattvas.

Request That the Wheel of Dharma Be Turned

Before the Lamps of the Worlds (the Buddhas)
of the ten directions,
Those who first Enlightenment won,
I now beseech them all
To turn the supremely wondrous wheel of Dharma.

Beseech the Buddhas to Remain in the World

If there are Buddhas who wish for Nirvana,
I beseech with deep sincerity
That they stay in the world for eons as many
as dust motes in worlds,
To benefit and bring happiness to every living being.

Always Follow the Buddhas and Learn From Them

All future Teachers of Gods and Humans (the Buddhas),
Whose quest for happiness has been fulfilled
I'll learn from and follow them
throughout the three periods of time,
And quickly attain great Enlightenment.

Always Comply With Living Beings

Ending their sufferings in the paths of evil,
And bringing happiness to everyone equally,
May I for eons like the particles of dust in a world
Ever benefit all in the ten directions.

Transfer All Merit to Living Beings

All the merit and virtue that I've acquired from
worshipping the Buddhas,
up to and including according with living beings,
I transfer to all living beings everywhere
Throughout the Dharma Realm and the reaches of space.[1]

[1] *Universal Worthy's Conduct and Vows,* Chapter 40, *Flower Adornment Sutra,* BTTS.

The Ideals Of The
Dharma Realm Buddhist Association

Members of the Dharma Realm Buddhist Association feel that it is extremely important for followers of the Dharma to maintain the high standards of ethics and practice originally taught by the Buddha. Although we may fall short of these standards, it is a mistake to dilute the teachings and bring them down to the level of our own personal inability and limited views. Rather we should recognize our faults and limitations and "try our best" to really change and go towards the ideal good as exemplified by the Buddhas and Bodhisattvas.

A Bodhisattva reflects to himself,

From beginningless kalpas in the past, because of greed, hatred and stupidity, in body, speech, and thought, I have created measureless, limitless bad karma. If this bad karma had a substance and appearance, exhausting the reaches of space it could not be contained within. I now completely purify my three karmas, and sincerely repent of all this before all the Buddhas and assemblies of Bodhisattvas throughout the Dharma Realm in world systems as numerous as the particles of dust in a world. I will never do any of it again, rather I will always abide in the merit and virtue of the pure moral precepts.[1]

The more we study the Sutras and actually practice the teachings, the more we become aware of how great our ignorance and faults are. Indeed, the key to genuine wisdom is the ability to see our ignorance and faults. For how can we solve the problem of our ignorance, the root of suffering, if we do not even realize to what extent it exists?

If we really have faith and some understanding of the Buddha's teachings, then, when we realize our faults, or when others point them out to us, we are truly happy, because we have the opportunity to change and go towards Enlightenment.

> *The Sage has few errors.*
> *The superior man changes his errors.*
> *The petty man covers his errors.*
> *The foolish man sees no errors.*[2]

No matter how great our faults are, or how obstructed we are by our greed, hatred, and delusion, we always have the potential to recognize this and change. One of the most remarkable things about the Dharma is that, although the criteria of the Buddha's ultimate purity and wisdom make our own state seem so coarse and impure by comparison, yet all of us still have the potential to become just like the Buddha.

The kindness of the Buddhas and Bodhisattvas is difficult to repay. If it were not for their great compassion we would not have the opportunity even to know about our true, enlightened nature, let alone the way to practice in order to realize it.

> *I am a good doctor for those who are suffering from sickness. I show the proper road to those who have lost their way. I am a bright light for those within the dark night. And I enable those who are poor to discover hidden treasures. A Bodhisattva in this way equally benefits all living beings....*
>
> *Why? Because all Buddhas, the Thus Come Ones, take a heart of great compassion as their substance. Because*

of living beings, they give rise to great compassion. From great compassion, the Bodhi-mind is born. Because of the Bodhi-mind they realize the Equal and Right Enlightenment.[3]

If we maintain the high standards of the Buddha's teachings, then we are giving ourselves and others the opportunity to realize the ultimate happiness and wisdom which come from studying and practicing them. The precious treasure of the Dharma must be carefully protected.

Activities Of The
Dharma Realm Buddhist Association

The Dharma Realm Buddhist Association (DRBA), formerly known as the Sino-American Buddhist Association, was established in 1959 as a state and federally approved non-profit religious and educational corporation for the purpose of bringing the orthodox teachings of the Buddha to the entire world.

At all of its monasteries, DRBA offers a rigorous schedule of Buddhist practice seven days a week from 4:00 a.m. to 10:00 p.m. The daily schedule includes approximately seven to eight hours of religious services, repentances, and group meditation, as well as lectures on the Buddhist scriptures. At the City of 10,000 Buddhas in Mendocino County, California the main training center of DRBA, there are also daily courses in Buddhist and canonical language studies, week-long intensive recitation and meditation sessions every other month, a month-long 10,000 Buddhas Repentance Ceremony in the spring (April/May), and a three to ten week Buddha recitation and Chan meditation session in the winter (December/January). Residents gain a thorough understanding of the essential teachings of the major schools of

117

Buddhism, develop skill in scriptural languages, and become adept at a wide variety of spiritual practices. The foundation of the practice is a high standard of ethics; all residents hold the Five Buddhist Precepts which prohibit killing any living being (includes vegetarianism), stealing, improper sexual conduct, false speech, and taking intoxicants (alcohol, drugs, and tobacco), and all strive to perfect the Six Guiding Principles: not contending with anyone, not being greedy, not seeking for anything, not being selfish, not wanting personal advantage, and not lying.

The activities of DRBA are offered through a federally approved four year Sangha (monastic) and four year Laity Training Program. The Sangha Training Program is partial fulfillment of requirements for receiving the Complete Precepts of a Bhikshu/Bhikshuni (celibate Buddhist monk/nun) through traditional ordination procedures. In 1972 DRBA held the first Complete Precept Platform in the United States at Gold Mountain Monastery in San Francisco. Since that time, the full ordination for Bhikshus and Bhikshunis has been held at the Sagely City of 10,000 Buddhas every three or four years.

One of DRBA's major tasks is the translation of the main Buddhist scriptures from Classical Chinese and Sanskrit into the world's languages, primarily English. To date, under the auspices of the Buddhist Text Translation Society, DRBA has published over 150 volumes in English, Chinese, Vietnamese and Spanish. Works in English include the *Flower Adornment (Avatamsaka) Sutra, Lotus Flower of The Wonderful Dharma (Saddharma-Pundarika) Sutra, Shurangama Sutra, Vajra Prajna Paramita (Diamond) Sutra, Sutra In 42 Sections, Great Compassion Heart Dharani Sutra of Avalokiteshvara Bodhisattva, Sutra of The Past Vows Of Earth Store (Kshitigarbha) Bodhisattva, Amitabha (Sukhavati-Vyuha)*

118

Sutra, Brahma Net Sutra, Sixth Patriarch's Sutra, 100 Dharmas Shastra, Shramanera Vinaya and Rules of Deportment, and Song of Enlightenment.

DRBA has established various educational and social service programs to promote peace, happiness, and a high standard of ethical conduct for the world. The Sagely City of 10,000 Buddhas also includes Dharma Realm Buddhist University, Developing Virtue Secondary School, and Instilling Goodness Elementary School. The elementary school emphasizes the development of reverence for one's parents; the secondary school stresses loyalty to one's country; and the university is based on the cardinal virtue of benevolence.

DRBA presently has branch monasteries in the United States in San Francisco, Los Angeles, Long Beach, Sacramento, San Jose and Seattle; in Canada in Vancouver and Calgary, as well as in Taiwan, Malaysia and Hong Kong.

The spiritual guide of DRBA is its founder, the most Venerable Tripitaka Master Hsuan Hua.

Dharma Realm Buddhist Association
City of Ten Thousand Buddhas
Dharma Realm Buddhist University

法界佛教總會
一萬佛聖城
法界佛教大學

The City of 10,000 Buddhas

[1]*Universal Worthy Bodhisattva's Conduct and Vows,* Chapter 40, *Flower Adornment Sutra,* BTTS.
[2]*Analects of Confucius.*
[3]*Universal Worthy Bodhisattva's Conduct and Vows,* Chapter 40, *Flower Adornment Sutra,* BTTS.

Index

A

Afflictions: 13, 20 Fn#1

Amitabha Buddha: *see* Pure Land

Arhats: 58-62, *see* Stream-enterer

Asankhyeya: 48 Fn# 14

B

Bhikshu & Bhikshuni: *see* Sangha

Bodhi-mind: 11, 2 Fn#7

Bodhisattva: ii-iv, 10, 29-30, 61-62, Ten Practices of 111-113

Buddha: i, v, Chapter Four 39-48, compassion 10-11, 41-42, Eighteen Exceptional Characteristics 45, mind-imprint, spiritual powers 43-44, Ten Powers 44-45, 60, Ten Titles 47, Thirty-two Hallmarks 45-47, Wisdom 42-43, 45

C

Chan (Dhyana/Zen): Chapter Six 71-81, four characteristics of 71, Four Dhyanas l04-105, meditation practice 75-81, transmission of 71, as unfixed teaching 72

Compassion: ii, 10-11, 15-16, 39, also *see* Buddha

D

Death: 8-11

Dharma: iii, ix Fn#3, 23-24, 33, 42-43, disappearance of 40-41, 58, 84

Dharma Realm: v, ix Fn#3

Dhyana: *see* Chan

Drinking & Drugs: 25

E

Eightfold Path: 23, Father-Reverence for Father & Mother: 27-30